How Power Works in Schools and Why It Matters for Maximizing Students' Learning

How Power Works in Schools and Why It Matters for Maximizing Students' Learning

Jacob W. Neumann

ROWMAN & LITTLEFIELD
Lanham • Boulder • New York • London

Published by Rowman & Littlefield
An imprint of The Rowman & Littlefield Publishing Group, Inc.
4501 Forbes Boulevard, Suite 200, Lanham, Maryland 20706
www.rowman.com
86-90 Paul Street, London EC2A 4NE, United Kingdom

Copyright © 2024 by Jacob W. Neumann

All rights reserved. No part of this book may be reproduced in any form or by any electronic or mechanical means, including information storage and retrieval systems, without written permission from the publisher, except by a reviewer who may quote passages in a review.

British Library Cataloguing in Publication Information Available

Library of Congress Cataloging-in-Publication Data

Names: Neumann, Jacob W., 1972– author.
Title: How power works in schools and why it matters for maximizing students' learning / Jacob W. Neumann.
Description: Lanham, Maryland: Rowman & Littlefield, 2024. | Includes bibliographical references. | Summary: "This book reveals the complex nature of power in schools and offers school leaders five actions that will help them more effectively manage power and better maximize students' learning"—Provided by publisher.
Identifiers: LCCN 2023044654 (print) | LCCN 2023044655 (ebook) | ISBN 9781475874112 (cloth) | ISBN 9781475874129 (paperback) | ISBN 9781475874136 (epub)
Subjects: LCSH: School management and organization—United States. | Educational leadership—United States. | School administrators—United States. | Teacher-administrator relationships—United States.
Classification: LCC LB2805 .N48 2024 (print) | LCC LB2805 (ebook) | DDC 371.200973—dc23/eng/20231027
LC record available at https://lccn.loc.gov/2023044654
LC ebook record available at https://lccn.loc.gov/2023044655

Contents

Preface	vii
Chapter 1: Defining Power in Schools	1
Chapter 2: Examining Power Philosophically	15
Chapter 3: Students' Power to Define Themselves	33
Chapter 4: The Tension between High-Stakes Testing and Teachers' Knowledge	55
Chapter 5: The Power of "Initiatives"	79
Chapter 6: The Problem of Consequences	97
Chapter 7: Why the "Big Stuff" Isn't the Biggest	119
Chapter 8: Work *with* Power to Maximize Students' Learning	131
Bibliography	153
About the Author	165

Preface

Power in schools has been analyzed starting at least since 1932, with George Counts's social reconstructionist tract *Dare the Schools Build a New Social Order?*[1] Power is almost only analyzed by what are called "critical" traditions in education scholarship, such as critical pedagogy and critical theory. These critical traditions try to use schools to change society for politically progressive, or Leftist, causes. One scholar describes them as "aimed at developing levels of critical consciousness among children and youth so that they become aware of the kinds of ills that the society has and become motivated to learn how to alleviate them."[2]

The problem with these kinds of scholarship is that they usually don't look outside of their political purpose and take account of schools in the school's terms, in the terms of the teachers, students, and principals actually working, learning, and struggling together inside classrooms and school buildings. Plus, they're almost never practical. Dense theoretical arguments often bear little resemblance to the daily struggles in schools. Lastly, they're usually wrong. Their claims about power are usually either politically driven, or they don't account for the full context within schools, which leaves those analyses, at best, lacking and, at worst, biased.

This book takes a different approach to analyzing how power works in schools. It uses the voices, experiences, and stories of students, teachers, and school leaders to make and illustrate its arguments. These stories provide high-resolution images, so to speak, of power as revealed by the language, decisions, actions, and emotions of real people in real contexts. The book doesn't address politics or try to make a political point. It doesn't address social movements. Nor does it address notions of how power "should" or "ought to" work in schools. Instead, it focuses on the practical, on how power actually works in schools.

The book develops the following core tenet: correctly understanding how power works in schools is crucial for maximizing students' learning. This tenet follows from a central understanding about power—that it is not a thing, that it's not linear and doesn't flow, that it exists everywhere, and that it acts like a web. Most people think of power incorrectly—mainly in terms of action and reaction—as in, the teacher told the students to hush, and they hushed. Of course, action/reaction power exists in schools (or teachers would never get their students to hush!). But that's not the only type of power in schools, nor is it the most important.

Consider the complexity of this core understanding. Power works like a web because it comes from everywhere and because the effects of each instance of power pull on the other instances of power in the web. Power is not linear, because it comes from everywhere and because it works like a web. Power is not a thing, because it comes from everywhere. The close connections here—even cause-and-effect connections—are not just repetition; they're fundamental to understanding the complicated and tightly interconnected ways that power works in schools.

How one thinks about power matters, even if that thinking is tacit (perhaps *because* it's tacit), because incorrect thinking leads to bad decision making. Since most people in and around schools get power wrong, they make decisions that make schools operate less than optimally and maintain barriers to teachers' teaching effectiveness. Here's one example: most people think that power flows from those in charge onto those being supervised, so it's no surprise that teachers are only invited to help solve classroom-level problems and seldom with system-level problems—which means that the school doesn't run as efficiently and optimally as it otherwise could.

The analysis in the book draws from decades of experience in teaching and research at all levels of schooling: extensive qualitative research in middle and high schools; university teacher preparation and supervision for elementary school teaching; doctoral teaching and dissertation supervision for teachers, curriculum specialists, principals, and other school leaders; and classroom teaching at every level.

The chapters in the book cover a wide range of topics from students' assessment of their "gifted and talented" ("GT") labels to the impact that school-based "initiatives" have on teachers' work. This diversity of topics illustrates how power impacts on a daily basis all areas of schooling from teaching to curriculum design to campus leadership and more. The following list briefly explains the contents of each chapter:

- Chapter 1 outlines the difficulties in correctly understanding power in schools, introduces the research context and methodology, and establishes the operational definition of power used throughout the book. This definition forms the outline for the rest of the book: "Power is not a thing, it is not linear, it comes from everywhere, and its effects work like a web."

- Chapter 2 digs deeply into the operational definition of power by looking closely at four of the main ways that people have thought about power throughout history. The chapter examines the major thinkers within each iteration of power and builds a detailed case for the operational definition as the most accurate and useful model for how power works in schools.
- Chapter 3 begins the book's empirical examination of power by illustrating how power is not a thing. The chapter analyzes power by looking at a subtle phenomenon: gifted and talented students' perceptions of their GT labels. It finds that students' power here challenges assumptions about GT labels, which can impact the quality of services that GT students receive.
- Chapter 4 shows how power is not linear. Contrary to popular opinion, power doesn't flow. It doesn't move in a line from one place to another. Instead, it emerges as people act and make decisions. The chapter looks at this aspect of power through a particular tension: the tension between mandated testing and teachers' knowledge and beliefs about teaching as the influences on how they teach.
- Chapter 5 demonstrates that not only is power not linear, but it also comes from everywhere. Chapter 5 makes this case by examining how "initiatives" are designed to both directly and indirectly impact how teachers teach. Further, and more importantly, the chapter shows how these initiatives have interacted with each other—not always productively, as they bounced around the educational landscape.
- Chapter 6 shows how, because power comes from everywhere in a school, it creates a sort of web within the school's landscape. Wherever power is exerted within the web, it pulls on other parts of the web, like a spider web being tugged by a breeze. Chapter 6 investigates this phenomenon with three school leaders, adding their perspectives to the students' and teachers' experiences already studied.
- Chapter 7 takes a step back to reiterate the case that the "small stuff" impacts schools as much as—and probably more than—the "big stuff." Using examples from chapters 3 through 6, the chapter analyzes two historically big influences on schools—high stakes testing and school reform—and illustrates why those big influences have been continuously ameliorated by the small stuff.
- Chapter 8 suggests five actions school leaders can take that work *with* power to maximize student learning. The actions focus on doing school *with* students and families, letting go of ego, predicting the future, emphasizing teachers' teaching effectiveness, and operationalizing the local community. These actions can help maximize students' learning

by removing obstacles, helping teachers teach to their strengths, and promoting family involvement.

The goal of the book is to provide school leaders (principals, teachers, curriculum specialists, and others) with the understanding and tools to recognize, analyze, and productively use power in their schooling contexts to maximize students' learning. The book does not argue that power always operates exactly as it does in these stories. No book can make such a claim. Power is too contextual, too malleable to personality and circumstance, to suggest one-size-fits-all rules. But this book does draw lessons for how power likely operates on a wider scale. The book makes this assertion because schools aren't that different across the country.

Small variations definitely exist from place to place: curriculum specifics change, test pressures vary, and so forth. But the basic organization of schooling stays the same from Oregon to Texas to Maine. Thus, education scholars don't write that schooling is fundamentally different in different parts of the country. Instead, similar pressures and challenges, for the most part, exist for educators wherever one goes. Thus, it's reasonable to not precisely generalize but to still imply general claims. Because even though the sample is small, it largely represents the experiences that educators across the US face, as schools are so similar.

Too often power is only an afterthought in schools, perhaps something to hopefully avoid or to unfortunately contend with when the next big issue arises and school leaders are forced to deal with it. This is a mistake. This is an ineffective and inefficient way of thinking about power. Power is always there; it's in all decisions, and everyone is always trying to exert it. But correctly understanding and being able to act with power makes all the difference. Instead of being an obstacle, power can become an ally—if you know how to work with it.

NOTES

1. George S. Counts, *Dare the school build a new social order?* (Carbondale, IL: Southern Illinois University Press, 1978).
2. See Elliot W. Eisner, *The educational imagination: On the design and evaluation of school programs*, 3rd ed. (Upper Saddle River, NJ: Prentice Hall, 2002), 76. Eisner wasn't espousing these beliefs. Instead, he was surveying purposes for education across society and identified this as one of those purposes.

Chapter 1

Defining Power in Schools

Power seems easy to understand. After all, there is no shortage of examples in life of what appear to be more powerful people imposing their will onto less powerful people. Perhaps it's the cruel boss, the tyrannical ruler, the corrupt public official, or maybe even the abusive parent. Whatever the specifics, most people seem to think that power flows downhill—that is, from more powerful people onto less powerful people, with those at the bottom usually bearing the brunt of its effects. At least that's the way it often looks.

Power in schools seems similarly simple. You're bound to see discussions of it on the news or on social media. They'll almost always involve people trying to advance an agenda: telling parents to mind their own business and stay out of curriculum decisions, trying to restrict what books kids read in schools, or imposing particular political beliefs into teaching decisions. Perhaps you heard about the gubernatorial debate in which one candidate said to the other, "I don't think parents should be telling schools what they should teach."[1] Or maybe you read about a Texas state representative's attempt to ban some 850 books from Texas public library shelves.[2]

These very public and attention-grabbing headlines represent how most people think about power in schools: as a blunt-force instrument that people use to impose their will onto others. And that's about it. That's about as far as thinking about power in schools commonly goes: it stays pretty simple. The flaw with this typical line of thinking, however, is that power in schools is not simple . . . at least not usually.

Sometimes, of course, power is simple and blunt. Sometimes it is about changing aspects of schooling in large and public ways. Sometimes it does seem like a zero-sum game, where people fight for the limited amounts of power that are available. After all, the law compels kids to attend school, and schools compel kids to do all sorts of activities—complete schoolwork, sit in assigned seats, keep quiet in class—whether they like it or not. And it's not just kids who feel the effects of power. Teachers feel pressured to cover content and effectively teach skills. Principals feel pressured to raise test scores across their schools.

But usually power in schools is far more complex, nuanced, and common. There is no zero-sum game for power in schools, at least not on a daily basis. The truth about power is that it is everywhere. Everyone has it. Nobody in schools is powerless, from students up to the district superintendent. Plus, it's always in action to the point that power is a phenomenon, not a tool. Power exists in daily decisions by teachers, within the minds of students, and even within the directives given by principals and other school leaders. These "little" decisions that people make in the daily course of schooling just to make schools run happen all the time.

It's been claimed that decisions about schooling are always exercises of power. That's true, but not in the way people making those claims likely intend. Decisions about schooling certainly can aim to advance particular agendas. But most decisions involve just trying to make the enterprise work: trying to best teach a class, to best figure out students' needs, to best lead a school, and more. It's those "little" decisions that are imbued with power as a phenomenon—something that just appears as people make day-to-day decisions within and about schools: teaching decisions, curriculum decisions, administrative decisions, funding decisions, and more.

It makes sense that most people misunderstand how power works in schools. Power in schools is complicated, and it can be hard to see, sometimes so hard that power might not even be thought of as power. But this is also a problem. It makes teaching, administering, and even researching in schools fraught with potential unintended consequences, hurting decision making, hurting teaching, and hurting school administration.

This is why correctly understanding how power works as a phenomenon inside schools is crucial for most effectively leading schools, teaching in classrooms, conducting educational research, and generating the most meaningful learning for students. Because power is misunderstood, because people usually don't see the web of power dynamics power creates across a school, its effects aren't anticipated and maybe not recognized, resulting in less effective policies and practices in schools.

Most importantly, misunderstanding how power works in schools helps keep students from maximizing their learning. Students' learning is impacted for two main reasons: schools focus on the wrong concerns (the big, public ones) instead of the ones that make the most impact (the small, daily ones), and teachers' effectiveness isn't maximized. Schools tend to focus on the big, easily visible things: high-stakes testing, school reform efforts, political actions, and so forth. Such actions, however, dissipate quickly, leaving the day-to-day still in place. And schools consistently erect obstacles to maximizing their teachers' effectiveness, even if they don't see it.

In response to this problem, this book develops the following claim about power: *Power in schools is not a thing, nor is it linear, because power comes from everywhere, and its effects pull on each other like a web*. Contrary to popular thinking, power doesn't work linearly, as in simple actions and reactions, and it doesn't flow downhill. Instead, it works more like a web in that power exerted from one place and on one thing can actually impact a range of different things across a school. Plus, it comes from many sources. Teachers and principals, of course, exert power. But, perhaps surprisingly, so can students. School initiatives even exert power.

This book examines power in schools not by looking at big, easily visible things but by carefully examining the little things. Easily visible examples of power include such actions as directives from state education agencies, providing or withholding funding for schools, teach-ins and sit-ins, students protesting by walking out of class, and so forth. While such actions can be important—or at least seem important—the power involved is not that complicated. It's mainly just an action trying to change someone else's behavior.

The little things, on the other hand, reveal the complexity and nuance of power in schools, and they illustrate each section of the book's central claim about power. To gain a sense of the nuanced nature of power, this book looks closely at small-scale phenomena within educators' schools and classrooms: students exerting power over their institutional labels, teachers exerting power over the scope and sequence of the curriculum they teach, school initiatives creating unanticipated consequences across a school, and school administrators negotiating the myriad dictates and obstacles enacted by the central office.

AN OPERATIONAL DEFINITION OF POWER

Before moving this analysis forward, an operational definition of power must be established. Opinions about the meaning and nature of power differ. While some people might see power as brute force, others will see it as molding or shaping. Still others might define power ideologically. Plenty of other definitions of power likely exist. Thus, it helps to share the same working understanding. An operational definition just means a definition given a particular context and particular circumstances.

Within the law, for example, the word *guilty* holds a specific meaning. In everyday language, people commonly use the word guilty to mean that a person definitely committed the act or the crime he's been charged with. But within the law, guilty does not mean that a person definitely did the act he is charged with. Instead, guilt involves *reasonable doubt*, which means that the members of a jury must think beyond a reasonable doubt that the defendant committed the act. This is a specific definition of the word guilty, one that requires an operational definition (which judges tell juries when they begin their deliberations on a case).

In a similar manner, what power means in schools also requires an operational definition. Four questions must be answered to create this definition:

1. How does power relate to brute force? What about coercion? Are they the same or different? How are people to distinguish between them? Do freedom of choice and action play a role in determining whether power exists? Can power exist without them?
2. What's the most useful image for describing how power acts? *Flow* is commonly used, as in "Power flows downhill." But is flow the correct metaphor, or is some other image more appropriate? Metaphors send particular signals; which one is most helpful?
3. Must power cause a change in someone's behavior? Does power even need to act on people, or can it show its effects differently? Put more specifically, can a decision be an example of exerting power, regardless of whether or not it directly affects other people?
4. Is power a thing that can be possessed and stored for future use? Do some people hold more power than others? The effects of power seem to be felt differently by different people; what accounts for that?

Question No. 1: Is Power the Same as Brute Force?

Is power the same as brute force? Put differently, what circumstances must exist for power to operate? Take an extreme example: a Nazi guard at a concentration camp. Guards had complete control over their prisoners. Prisoners had no liberty, no option to refuse commands. They also had no oversight board to complain to, no warden, no bureau of prisons, no state legislator, no congressional representative, no local newspaper, and no visitors that might help them with a complaint. If concentration camp prisoners refused to comply with a guard's commands, they risked immediate death, likely from being shot on the spot.

What about another extreme example, enslaved people in the American South prior to the Civil War? A plantation owner who enslaved others, similar to a concentration camp guard, controlled almost all aspects of enslaved people's lives. Any enslaved people who refused to follow a plantation owner's or overseer's commands had no means of recourse. They risked (usually) not death but severe beatings or other harsh physical punishments.

So given the context and the consequences prisoners faced if they refused to comply, were a concentration camp guard's commands exercises of power? What about the plantation owner or overseer and the degree to which they controlled enslaved people's lives? Or were the guard's and overseer's commands simply a use of brute force? This distinction between power and brute force comes from the philosopher Michel Foucault.

Foucault argues that "there is no power without potential refusal or revolt."[3] According to Foucault, "if an individual can remain free, however little his freedom may be," power can exist, and "a man who is chained up and beaten is subject to force being exerted over him, not power."[4] Concentration camp prisoners and enslaved people weren't continually chained and beaten, at least not literally. But the context is certainly similar regarding the degree of control over almost every aspect of their lives and the ramifications they faced for noncompliance.

Foucault then tells us that concentration camp guards and enslavers did not exercise power—they used brute force. Following Foucault, we find power and brute force are not the same. And freedom, even the smallest amount, Foucault argues, is the quality that makes the difference. For power to exist, people must be free to refuse compliance. This doesn't mean that they won't suffer because of their noncompliance. For example, local governments exercise taxation power over residents. Residents are free to not pay, say, their property taxes, but they might lose or surrender their property as a consequence.

So power is not the same as brute force. Plus, in schools, students, teachers, and principals have freedom. They can choose not to follow commands. They can choose not to follow rules. They might suffer unpleasant, even severe, consequences for noncompliance, but the situation is wholly different from the concentration camp and plantation examples. Students might receive low grades, perhaps even get expelled. Teachers and principals can lose their jobs. That's serious but certainly not life-threatening.

Question No. 2: What's the Most Useful Image for Describing How Power Acts?

People often describe power in terms of *flow*. For example, power seems to flow downhill, from "more powerful" people (such as an employer) to "less powerful" people (such as employees). This flow of power seems easy to see in schools: superintendents dictate to principals, who dictate to teachers, who dictate to students. Indeed, a big part of schooling consists of responding to directions from others. Years ago, researchers identified this "top down" movement as "the conduit," a sort of channel which funnels commands and directives down to teachers and administrators from "on high."[5]

But is flow the most accurate or meaningful metaphor to describe how power acts? For starters, the metaphor quickly gets complicated. If power "flowing" from, say, school district administrators all the way to students is labeled as flowing downhill, then how should one describe power coming from students—as flowing uphill? And what about from one teacher to another—as flowing sideways?

To ask if power flows is akin to asking if power operates linearly. The short answer is no. To operate linearly means to work or function in a line along a constrained or focused path, in a sequential process, in a recognizable step-by-step fashion. It means that power is directed from one place or person to another. A linear operation is somewhat predictable in that paths can be traced, allowing past action to at least nominally predict future action. *Linearly* also implies movement along that line. Thus, asking if power operates linearly also asks if power flows.

Perhaps some simple metaphors can prove useful in further analyzing this question. Rivers, electrical currents, and water and air currents are all phenomena that flow. What do they reveal about how power might flow? These examples demonstrate three different types of flow. The first type is unidirectional. Rivers and direct electrical current flow in one direction. They show current flowing from a source to a destination (as in the case of rivers, perhaps a lake or larger body of water, and in the case of direct current, back to the original power source). Their flow can be measured and is largely consistent.

Second, water and air currents also flow in one direction, but their path is much less defined than rivers or direct current. The paths of water and air currents curve due to wind and air pressure, creating large spirals. These spirals shift position but, depending on the scale, can remain relatively stable. The third is alternating current. Alternating current flows forwards and backwards, changing direction very rapidly many times a second. This current still follows a prescribed path, and it can be measured.

So does power operate in schools like any of these examples? No. Power doesn't move in straight lines from one person or place to another. It doesn't follow any prescribed paths. It isn't predictable or measurable. And power only sometimes acts toward a destination, but it just as frequently acts without any particular path or target. In fact, power can't really be said to flow or move at all. Power certainly operates in schools, but it operates somewhat randomly. It emerges or is exerted as circumstances change and people make decisions as they live and act.

A more useful metaphor for describing how power works in schools is a web. Foucault argues that a network of power relations forms "a dense web that passes through apparatuses and institutions."[6] With a spiderweb, pulling on any one string pulls, at least a little bit, on all of the other strings. Whenever power is exerted in or related to schools, it is thought to emerge within the web. It lights up, so to speak, and pulls on the web, creating multiple reactions across the web.

Question No. 3: Must Power Cause a Change in Someone's Behavior?

How can one know when power exists or when it has been exerted? What evidence can be used? Must it cause a change in someone's behavior, or does other evidence of it exist? A recent definition posits power as "the ability to influence another's behavior."[7] This is an action/reaction definition of power. In this case, power is the action, and the change in someone else's behavior is the reaction.

Such thinking about power likens it to a force in physics, which is defined as an action or influence that changes the motion of an object. In physics, if a boy pushes on a rock and moves the rock, he creates a force on the rock by changing its position. However, if the boy pushes on the rock but doesn't move it, regardless of how hard he pushes, he does not create a force on that rock. So in physics, for a force to exist, the thing being acted upon must react to the acting agent. In the case of the rock, no force is created if the rock just sits there.

Action/reaction thinking about power seems to suggest a similar relationship. It seems to suggest that unless someone's behavior is influenced—that is, changed—then power does not exist. Yet is this the most useful or accurate definition of power as related to schooling? Does it cover all possible contingencies and circumstances when power might exist? Further, is it necessary that someone influence a *person's* behavior?

Consider the following two examples. In the first example, a teacher tells a student to stop talking during a lesson, and the student stops talking (quite often, teachers must tell students multiple times, sometimes even raising their voices, which can make it seem much more authoritarian). This is a clear action/reaction example: the teacher exerted power and changed the student's behavior. Indeed, this example might represent prototypical thinking about power in schools. It's top down, it's easily visible, and it's common.

But now consider a different example, one in which a teacher revises the scope and sequence for a section of the curriculum for her sixth-grade social studies class. Instead of following the school district's curriculum guidelines for how to structure and teach units on, say, Central and South America, the teacher follows her knowledge, experience, and insight and revises that curriculum plan into a pattern she thinks will better serve her students. Did the teacher exert power?

According to the action/reaction definition from above, perhaps she did not. The teacher did not influence the curriculum writer's behavior. Nor did she change her colleagues' or her administrators' behaviors. She influenced her students' behavior, but she would have done that with either curriculum plan—the prescribed one or her revised version. It does not seem reasonable, however, to suggest that the teacher did not exert power. But if the teacher did not exert power *on a person*, how did the teacher exert power?

In this case, the teacher exerted power *on the situation*, on the teaching and curriculum decision with which she contended. In this case, the teacher was given a specific curriculum plan, which is a sort of directive from the school district about what content to teach, in what order, and for how long. Not only did this teacher not follow the directive, she didn't ask for permission to change the plan. She just did it.

This happens often in schools. Teachers routinely change policies such as district curriculum guidelines, school reform efforts, and even initiatives enacted by school principals. And in most cases, teachers don't seek permission to make changes—they don't exert power to try to change someone's mind. Instead, like the sixth-grade social studies teacher, they just make the change within the confines of their classrooms. In these varied instances, teachers exert power by influencing pedagogical situations.

An action/reaction definition of power fails to capture this crucial difference. In education, sometimes power emerges as the changing of someone's behavior or thinking. But lots of other times, power emerges more subtly, such as the example of the teacher changing school district curriculum plans. So in schools, the evidence suggests that power must change educational situations or circumstances. That power might emerge through changing someone's thinking or, perhaps, even emerge as a decision someone makes related to teaching, curriculum, or another schooling topic.

Question No. 4: Is Power a Thing That Can Be Possessed and Stored for Future Use?

People commonly think that power is a "thing," something that small numbers of people possess but most do not or, perhaps, that people possess in different amounts. In this line of thinking, power can be accumulated, stored, and used whenever necessary. Schools, parents, the general public, and even students themselves often think that students possess no power. Teachers also often see themselves as powerless. And both students and teachers often see principals as possessing all the power in schools (an assertion that principals would definitely dispute).

But what would this mean? What would it look like for power to be a thing? If power were a thing, it could be taken away. Because hierarchies of power operate in schools, those with more power could take away power from less powerful people. Since students sit at the bottom of the hierarchy, teachers and administrators could easily take power from students. Or they could limit or ration students' ability to use their power by putting restrictions and conditions on its use.

Complications, however, quickly arise in thinking about power as a thing. Some complications can be framed humorously, such as where one would keep power. After all, power can't be packed into a box and stored in a closet. It can't be measured out and dispensed over, say, a week (this much on Monday, this much on Tuesday, etc.). And if someone can keep power, can power also be misplaced? Imagine: "Honey, have you seen my power? I had it here a moment ago?"

Further, according to Foucault, "power is not a substance;" instead, "power is only a certain type of relation between individuals."[8] In this line of thinking, power is not a thing but a type of interaction between people. As Foucault puts it, "Power exists only as exercised by some on others."[9] Contrary to Foucault's thought on this second point, however, this book will argue that power doesn't exist only as a dynamic between people. The logic behind this position is found, of course, in the response to chapter 3. The label "power" must apply to an individual's ability to influence educational situations, which greatly expands the meaning of power.

And power doesn't run out. There is no well of power that can run dry. Teachers, say, always have the ability to influence and shape their teaching. Thus, they always have the ability to exert power over their teaching, even in the smallest of ways. That power can't be taken away from them, even in highly scripted classrooms. It's always there. People exert power differently, of course. But that doesn't mean some people have more of it than others. It just means that differential effects can be felt depending on the context in which power is exerted.

An Operational Definition

The preceding analysis combines to form an operational definition of power for this book: *Power is an action, not a thing or commodity, that influences or shapes the nature of an education situation, and that manifests not as a linear "flow" but as part of a web of other power relations within the landscape of a school or other educational context*. So, the operational definition of power is essentially the same as the premise for the book.

This analysis helps visualize power as a phenomenon that is created organically as people interact and make decisions. To study power phenomenologically means, put simply, to study it as a phenomenon that is a part of experience. Or as Max Van Manen put it, "Phenomenology asks the simple question, what is it like to have a certain experience?".[10] Here experience means an everyday occurrence. Recognizing the commonplace nature of power demystifies it and enables analysis of everyday language and decisions as generators of power.

To consider power as a phenomenon is to think about it as both big and small. Big is easy to see. Those are the pronouncements, the initiatives, the legislation, the blue-ribbon committees, the large-scale grants, and so forth. This book, however, focuses on the small. Small focuses on individual people's language, actions, experiences, and decisions. The big happens only sometimes. The small happens all the time. And students do this daily, as do teachers and principals, when they decide how to implement a curriculum plan, operationalize central office directives, and so forth.

Big power might seem more important, precisely because it's easier to see. Small power, on the other hand, hides itself behind classroom and office doors, making it much harder to see—and, consequently, much harder to measure, gauge, or estimate. While the big is certainly important, this book argues that the small is at least as important—and probably more so—because of the consistent impacts it makes on the daily teaching, learning, and leading that goes on inside schools. Put differently, big power makes claims about how school will change, while small power works to actually change schools.

A BRIEF DESCRIPTION OF THE PARTICIPANTS AND THE RESEARCH METHODOLOGY

This book looks at power by carefully examining the experiences of educators from different parts of Texas (as well as some of their students). Chapters 3, 4, and 5 focus on four middle school social studies teachers: Margaret Rhodes, Bill Trammell, Mary Watson, and Orlando Gaines. They taught at Connors Middle School, which is located in the Rio Grande Valley in South Texas. Chapter 6 focuses on three other educators who work as school supervisors in other parts of Texas: Hector Resendez, Tomas Gracia, and Lionel Avila.[11]

The research supporting this book is grounded in narrative inquiry. Narrative inquiry is ideally suited to investigate power because, as well-known narrative researchers put it, "The principal attraction of narrative as a research method is its capacity to render life experiences, both personal and social, in relevant and meaningful ways;"[12] in this case, it is the teachers,' administrators,' and students' experiences with and around power in schools.

Narrative inquiry is a form of qualitative research that investigates peoples' experiences as they live them, using their own words and honoring their own feelings and perceptions of those experiences. Narrative inquiry is "concerned with the meanings people construe of their lived experiences in context" and with understanding and representing those meanings in their terms—as opposed to the researcher's terms.[13] The task of narrative researchers is not to impose external guidelines or conditions on a research project but to work with research participants to elicit what they know and are finding in professional practice.

Narrative inquiry shares many of the same attributes as other approaches to qualitative research. Researchers go to school sites or other educational settings; they sit off to the side and watch, listen, take notes, and take audio recordings of everyday classroom activities. They interview teachers or other school personnel. They collect documents or other artifacts that represent what happened in the classroom.

However, narrative inquiry differs from other forms of qualitative research in that narrative can be thought of as a storytelling form of research, as it seeks to explore and tell people's stories as they live and experience them. Narrative recognizes that people live storied lives. People don't just exist. They compose stories about their lives as they live them. Those stories can help as well as hurt. Helpful stories provide cohesion and direction to people's lives, while hurtful stories erect obstacles and doubt. And people's stories change over time as they gain new experiences or reflect on old ones.

In narrative inquiry, "story forms both the source of information through storytelling as well as the vehicle for interpretation and reinterpretation of experience."[14] According to Connelly and Clandinin, "people are both living their stories in an ongoing experiential text and telling their stories in words as they reflect upon life and explain themselves to others."[15] The educators in this study told stories about their work, as they continuously lived stories in their classrooms. In turn, this book tells stories of those stories as the vehicle for conveyance and analysis.

Indeed, stories might sit at the core of narrative inquiry as researchers learn, live, and tell teachers' cover, secret, and sacred stories.[16] Cover stories are the stories teachers tell about their work in public, out-of-classroom spaces, stories that fit within the "acceptable" range of the story of school being lived in the school. Teachers tell secret stories, on the other hand, mainly to each other or to trusted friends or other colleagues. Secret stories are the real stories, the actual stories of practice and experience that teachers live every day. Last, sacred stories are told *to* teachers. They are filled with other people's visions of what is "right" for children.

Because of this emphasis on story, narrative researchers emphasize relationship and trust. Those relationships involve "mutual storytelling and restory-ing as the research proceeds."[17] Thus, this method "is a collaboration between a researcher and participants, over time, in a place or series of places, and in social interaction with milieus."[18] The goal of the narrative endeavor is to get past the cover stories and into the secret stories, the truer truths. This process takes time, time to build relationships and time to build trust between the researchers and the person being "researched."

Two assumptions operate here: (1) people don't tell their secret stories to just anybody, and (2) narrative researchers think they can discern secret stories from cover stories. The first assumption is easily supported. Who tells the "truest truth" to strangers or to people they don't fully trust? Probably nobody does. Who tells an employer an unvarnished truth? Also, there are likely few. You're likely to tell your boss what you think he or she wants to hear (a cover story), not what is necessarily the truest truth (the secret story)—unless you feel confident in the level of trust in your relationship. But even then, it feels risky.

The second assumption carries more uncertainty and connects to concerns about trustworthiness and lifelikeness for readers. How can researchers know when or if they hear a secret story? Sometimes gut reactions play a role. Does the story feel true? How does the story relate to other bits of evidence or other stories the researcher has collected, heard, or seen? How consistent are the stories? How open, honest, and perhaps even vulnerable does the utterance feel? Indeed, Craig claims that ultimately, "it is readers . . . who determine the trustworthiness of [a] research endeavor."[19]

Narrative inquiry's emphasis on trust and relationship troubles the common labels used within qualitative research. For example, in most ways of thinking about qualitative research, either a *participant observer* or a *nonparticipant observer* goes to a school or other such research site to observe and investigate one or more research "participants." Think of a participant observer as someone like a teacher researching her own class while she teaches it. A nonparticipant observer, on the other hand, researches events without taking an active role in those events. These observers study *participants*, people who agree to being studied.

These formal terms—participant, participant observer, and nonparticipant observer—technically apply to narrative inquiry, but they don't fit in spirit. Teachers, for example, agree to participate, but they aren't abstract entities to dispassionately and remotely study. Teachers live experiences inside classrooms, and researchers, to the extent they can, live those experiences with them. Then, when they talk together, they tell and retell those experiences with each other, making sense of them along the way.

Similarly, nonparticipant observer, which technically describes most narrative inquirers, doesn't really work either. It's too distant, implying a lack of relationship. Even the term *observation* feels wrong. Yes, narrative researchers observe, but it's more like they spend time in classrooms (or whichever settings) as colleagues, often as friends. Not that they begin projects as friends. In all likelihood, they'll begin as strangers. But over time, they often develop friendships from the time spent together, the honest conversations, and the common goal of making sense of their experiences.

NOTES

1. Matthew Impelli, "McAuliffe saying parents shouldn't tell schools what to teach big factor in election: Poll," *Newsweek*, November 5, 2021, https://www.newsweek.com/mcauliffe-saying-parents-shouldnt-tell-schools-what-teach-big-factor-election-poll-1649488.

2. Bill Chappell, "A Texas lawmaker is targeting 850 books that he says could make students feel uneasy," NPR, published October 28, 2021, https://www.npr.org/2021/10/28/1050013664/texas-lawmaker-matt-krause-launches-inquiry-into-850-books.

3. Michel Foucault, *Power*, ed. James D. Faubion (New York: The New Press, 2000), 324.

4. Foucault, *Power*, 324.

5. D. Jean Clandinin and F. Michael Connelly, "Teachers' professional knowledge landscapes: Teacher stories. Stories of teachers. School stories. Stories of school," *Educational Researcher* 25, no. 3 (1996): 24.

6. Michel Foucault, *The history of sexuality: An introduction*, vol. 1, trans. Robert Hurley (New York: Vintage Books, 1990), 96.

7. Julie Battilana and Tiziana Casciaro, *Power for all: How it really works and why it's everyone's business* (New York: Simon & Schuster, 2021), x.

8. Foucault, *Power*, 324.

9. Foucault, *Power*, 340.

10. Max Van Manen, "Phenomenological pedagogy," *Curriculum Inquiry* 12, no. 3 (1982): 296.

11. Pseudonyms are used for the names of all the educators. At this writing, they have a combined total of 157 years of experience: Margaret–37 years, Mary–30 years, Orlando–22 years, Bill–20 years, Hector–18 years, Tomas–17 years, and Lionel–13 years.

12. F. Michael Connelly and D. Jean Clandinin, "Stories of experience and narrative inquiry," *Educational Researcher* 19, no. 5 (1990): 10.

13. Cheryl J. Craig, "The contested classroom space: A decade of lived educational policy in Texas schools," *American Educational Research Journal* 46, no. 4 (December 2009): 1039.

14. Cheryl J. Craig, "Stories of schools/teacher stories: A two-part invention on the walls theme," *Curriculum Inquiry* 30, no. 1 (2000): 13.

15. Connelly and Clandinin, "Stories of experience," 4.

16. Connelly and Clandinin, "Teachers' professional knowledge landscapes: Teacher stories," 25.

17. Connelly and Clandinin, "Stories of experience," 4.

18. F. Michael Connelly and D. Jean Clandinin, "Narrative understandings of teacher knowledge," *Journal of Curriculum and Supervision* 15, no. 4 (Summer 2000): 20.

19. Cheryl J. Craig, "Coming to know in the 'eye of the storm': A beginning teacher's introduction to different versions of teacher community," *Teaching and Teacher Education* 29 (January 2013): 30.

Chapter 2

Examining Power Philosophically

Chapter 1 defined power in schools as actions that influence educational situations. But how do you really know that definition works? And why use that particular definition in the context of schools? Plenty of philosophers have written about power over the years. How does this definition hold up historically when compared against those other ideas? Why not just say that power in schools works the same way as power in any other context? Are definitions of power flexible, able to be molded to fit nuanced circumstances? Or should one consistent definition of power be applied to all situations?

Think about how a rock is defined. Defining what a rock is would seem pretty simple. They are, after all, rocks—things that people sweep off of their driveways. But rocks have different definitions depending on how they were created and what substances are inside them, such as with igneous, metamorphic, and sedimentary rocks. So defining a rock turns out to be not so simple. A rock is not a rock is not a rock; there isn't one consistent definition to encompass all varieties of rocks. So how could power, which is a social phenomenon, be expected to have one unitary definition when even rocks, which are naturally created, hold multiple definitions?

Power has been given an assortment of definitions because it occurs in different contexts, with different types of people, and with varying results. The concept of power has received so much attention throughout history that it's difficult to fully capture the full range of philosophers' thinking about it. While many thinkers focus on power within the political realm, most philosophers seem to consider power in terms of individual people working to achieve specific goals, often at the expense of *other* people's goals and desires. Yet philosophers have also argued for power in a variety of other terms.

It's useful to briefly examine some of these different opinions about power while making a case about how power works in schools. The following sections explain and describe differences between major thinkers' takes on power. The categories, while organized around certain philosophers, are not arranged by any type of ranking. Instead, they are arranged to tell a narrative that will reveal itself as the chapter progresses. The chapter ends by comparing and contrasting these categories against the facts of schooling to determine which is the most useful way of thinking about power in that context.

CATEGORIES OF THINKING ABOUT POWER

Thinking about power as an action, as something that occurs, as something that can be called upon and exerted, is so prevalent across societies that it can be hard to *not* think of power in those terms and to imagine that power could somehow be otherwise. Some philosophers do just that, though. How philosophers think about power isn't fixed. Some consider power in ways far different from the typical power-over-someone thinking. So to ask what it is that occurs when power operates is perhaps the wrong question. For some philosophers, nothing happens. For some, in fact, power is not even a verb.

This chapter groups thinking about power into four categories. These categories range from the individual to the collective to the almost metaphysical:

1. Action intended to change other people's behaviors
2. Collaboration creating the possibility of action
3. The basic, fundamental motivation for all human behavior
4. Action embedded within relational networks

These categories don't represent all of the different ways that philosophers have thought about power, but they do capture the most common and impactful thinking about power in the West over the past few centuries.

1. Action Intended to Change Other People's Behaviors

The most common way of thinking about power, the way most people seem to think about power, usually involves force, domination, or coercion. Essentially, in this line of thinking, power involves making people do what you want them to. Whether people want to oblige or not matters little; simple compliance is what counts. You see this understanding of power throughout pop culture ("Fight the power") and political discourse (amassing and spending political power). Even the hit TV show *Yellowstone* had a character define power this way to a classroom full of her students while making the point that she possessed power but that they did not.

This thinking about power stretches back centuries. A 2021 book by two business school professors defines power as "the ability to influence another's behavior, be it through persuasion or coercion."[1] A 1993 definition by the noted psychologist Mihaly Csikszentmihaly called power "the generic term to describe the ability of a person to have others extend their lives to satisfy his or her goals."[2] The philosopher Max Weber, in 1978, described power as "the possibility of forcing one's own will on the behavior of others."[3] According to Weber, power means asserting one's will within social relationships, even against the opposition of others.[4]

Much further back, in 1660, the philosopher Thomas Hobbes, in his book *Leviathan*, described power as the ability to secure well-being or personal advantage to obtain a future good. For Hobbes, power was relative: if one person had more, someone else had to have less. This is the same sort of zero-sum thinking about power described by twentieth-century philosopher C. Wright Mills. According to Mills, power exists in fixed amounts, and there is only so much to go around. Thus, for Mills, "any gain of power on the part of A must by definition occur by diminishing the power on the part of . . . B, C, D."[5]

According to British philosopher Bertrand Russell (1872–1970), this form of power has played an essential role in human history. He argues that people cannot correctly interpret history unless they first recognize that love of power has caused almost all important social actions throughout history. For Russell, "love of power is the chief motive producing the changes which social science has to study."[6] Russell emphasizes this claim by stating that love of power is a characteristic of people who are "causally important."[7]

Yet Russell has not claimed that power is the sole human motive. The love of power isn't spread evenly among people. Russell claims that almost everyone loves bits of power, power over particular parts of their lives, but not over every part of their life. A high-ranking executive might exert domination at the office but not at home. A local sheriff might enjoy power in the community but not on a statewide or national level. Some avoid power because they love ease, pleasure, or approval. Others avoid power out of timidity, "which . . . limits the desire for self-direction."[8]

Probably the most well-known (and perhaps the most notorious) example of this way of thinking about power comes from Niccolo Machiavelli in his book *The Prince*.[9] Originally published posthumously, way back in 1531, *The Prince* turned Machiavelli's name into an adjective: Machiavellian. Many scholars have noted the dangers surrounding power. Russell, for example, claims that love of power is dangerous to teachers because teachers must care for their students. And Nietzsche, while he recognizes despots' will to power, encourages more morally and socially productive uses of power. Machiavelli, however, offers no such warning.

Machiavelli wrote *The Prince* as a gift for Lorenzo de Medici, the ruler of Florence (in Italy) at the end of the fifteenth century. The Medici family had ruled Florence previously but were defeated and forced from power.

Machiavelli worked for the new Florentine Republic. When the Medici family soon returned to power, Machiavelli gifted *The Prince* to Lorenzo with the hopes of regaining favor and working for the Medicis.

The Prince was written as a type of power manual for Lorenzo. Within it, Machiavelli describes actions a ruler must take given a wide mix of circumstances, and he provides historical examples to illustrate his key points. Machiavelli doesn't just describe one or a few methods for gaining and keeping power—he describes many: find the particular circumstances and locate suggested actions. In this way, power, for Machiavelli, seems to be a tool that can be wielded more or less effectively, with some actions, depending on circumstances, being more useful than others.

For example, Machiavelli discusses how to conquer and rule different types of principalities (hereditary, composite, ecclesiastical, etc.); coming to power through fortune, through force, or through crime; and whether fortresses are useful. He discusses princes' behavior, why to shun flatterers, and how to win honor. He also analyzes wider civic and historical affairs, such as why Italian princes lost their principalities and how "to liberate Italy from the barbarians."[10]

While the term *Machiavellian* has been defined as "cunning, scheming, and unscrupulous," Machiavelli doesn't solely promote mean, hurtful, or duplicitous behavior.[11] He actually favors positive, uplifting actions. Machiavelli writes that having a reputation for compassion is better than having a reputation for cruelty.[12] He writes that leaders should endeavor "to escape being hated"[13] and to work hard "to win the reputation of being a great man of outstanding ability."[14] And he condemns treachery, stating that "it cannot be called prowess to kill fellow citizens, to betray friends, to be treacherous, pitiless, irreligious."[15]

Machiavelli emphasizes practical advice. He argues that it is best for a prince to be both loved and feared, but if both aren't possible, then fear is best, as well as that friendship bought with money and not with greatness doesn't last. He also says that miserliness is a vice that can sustain one's rule. Yet, and here is likely the cause of his negative reputation, Machiavelli does not avoid harsh, even brutal, advice. For example, he states that within particular conditions, "men must either be pampered or crushed" and that "any injury a prince does a man should be of such a kind that there is no fear of revenge."[16]

That's practical. If you must hit a man, hit him so hard that he won't strike back—practical but brutal. See, for Machiavelli, power was just a tool to be used to keep a prince in power. That was it. The ends justified the means. Power wasn't good or bad; it was either effective or ineffective. Machiavelli preferred for power not to hurt people. But his advice to Lorenzo didn't prioritize that feeling. Instead, it simply gave Lorenzo a full accounting of the potential range of actions he might take to maintain his station as prince.

2. Collaboration Creating the Possibility of Action

This next line of thinking about power emphasizes collective action. Unlike power as force, here power does not instrumentalize other people's behavior. Instead, it involves the formation of a *common* will in the attempt to reach agreement. This line of thinking prioritizes open, unfiltered, unrestricted, uncorrupted communication because, it is argued, only this type of communication can produce true and honest agreement. And free agreement is crucial because it allows the social system "to get things done in the interest of collective goals."[17]

In this second line of thinking, power can't be possessed. It can't be won. It can't even really be used, at least not in a strategic, measured, "be sure not to use all of your power" kind of way. For German philosopher Hannah Arendt (1906–1975), power doesn't belong to individuals. Instead, "it belongs to a group and remains in existence only so long as the group keeps together."[18] The word *belong* requires attention lest anyone think Arendt has referred to possession. Here it more precisely symbolizes being created by a group, formed by a group's free association and collaboration.

Power, following Arendt, closely connects to language. According to Arendt, "power can be reduced almost entirely to the qualities of speech understood as conversation within the transcendental horizon of language."[19] This means that power makes action possible, initially in the form of conversations. Think for a moment about conversations. Nobody owns a conversation as long as that conversation isn't dominated or highjacked by one person. They can start at any time, so the potential for conversation always exists. And they can last for as long as the participants decide to talk, theoretically even forever, if the participants could keep up.

The phrase "the horizon of possible activity" nicely frames this power/language/action relationship.[20] Conversation is one of the first steps in bringing people together to act in public. Conversation—as a form of public action—initiates the potential for things to happen: for decisions to get made, for plans to form, for efforts to be coordinated. This, for Arendt, is power. But it's power to get things done, not power over anyone. This power as potential also means the potential for something new to be created. This potential for new creation isn't limited a priori; in other words, it's a potential that stretches to the horizon.

For Arendt, possibility is what turns power into power instead of into force or violence. And the more open, free, and unrestricted the conversation, the more possibility the conversation holds—and the more power. Here you see how Arendt values freedom. Instead of power as imposition, Arendt articulates power as contingent on freedom. Indeed, Arendt "understands power as the ability to agree upon a common course of action in unconstrained communication."[21] So power for Arendt doesn't require particular results. It doesn't matter if things *do* happen; it matters if things *can* happen through unconstrained agreement.

Agreement here is based on conviction. Conviction applies in two ways to Arendt's thinking: (1) as the resulting belief, the agreement stemming from conversation; and (2) as the prior intent to use language "illocutionarily" (as a linguist might put it)—"that is, for the noncoercive establishment of intersubjective relations."[22] In other words, power begins with the action and the conviction of people trying to reach agreement instead of their own individual success.

Both the first and this second line of thinking connect power to politics. For the first, imagine a politician, say Lyndon Johnson, leaning into someone, perhaps physically intimidating that person, to achieve a desired goal. That's power as imposition. For Arendt, as well as for the philosopher Talcott Parsons (1902–1979), power also connects to politics. Arendt calls power "the medium of the originary political being together of human beings in action."[23] And Parsons describes power as a sort of "circulating medium" in which people can come together and agree on action.[24]

Some may object, of course, that politics is often pursued as a zero-sum game with winners and losers. For Arendt, such maneuvering would likely turn power into force. Commandeering a decision or a process, just like commandeering a conversation, moves a group away from unrestricted participation. Further, when politics reverts to force, the horizon of possible activity diminishes. Free conversation ceases, and language becomes directive instead of generative. In this sense, power is strong because it is creative, but it's also fragile because of how easily it can be corrupted into force. People, then, must work continually to maintain it.

3. The Basic, Fundamental Motivation for All Human Behavior

Perhaps the most unique conceptualization of power has been offered by Friedrich Nietzsche. Nietzsche, a German philosopher who lived from 1844 to 1900, is likely most popularly known for his aphorism "What doesn't kill me makes me stronger." Nietzsche wrote prolifically, spanning some twenty-seven books that include well-known titles such as *Beyond Good and Evil, Thus Spoke Zarathustra,* and *On the Genealogy of Morals.* His thinking addressed a wide range of subjects, including art, history, religion, philology, tragedy, science, and culture. Nietzsche didn't focus his books directly on power but spread his ideas on power across them.

Nietzsche's thinking about power utilized the phrase "will to power." For Nietzsche, the will to power is human beings' major motivator and source of human value. He held that "all driving force is will to power, that there is no other physical, dynamic, or psychic force except this."[25] This will to power is not simply a will to gain power, to become a ruler, or to wield control over others. Instead, it is "a desire to experience our own *power* in the broadest sense of that term, that is, to experience all of our various capabilities, capacities, or strengths, be they physical, mental, social, creative, intellectual, or practical."[26]

This notion of a will to power requires some unpacking. Power, here, is a personal power. It is experienced through the fulfillment of one's ultimate desire. By his use of *ultimate*, Nietzsche contrasts against proximate desires, which are temporary means to attain something else. Money, for example, is a proximate desire because of the things and lifestyle it can buy. Ultimate desires, on the other hand, hold value for their own sake, as ends in themselves. An ultimate desire might be socially objectionable, or it might be laudable. It might involve, say, the subjugation of others. Or it might be artistic, such as the desire to create and share beautiful music.

Where, one might ask, does power come from in fulfilling an ultimate desire? While Nietzsche used the phrase "will to power" in his writing, a more accurate rendering of this sentiment is "the will to the experience of power."[27] But this, too, requires explanation, for how does one find power in the experience of power if, by "power," one means the fulfillment of an ultimate desire? The answer has to do with resistance. Ultimate desires aren't easy to satisfy; something always resists. Nietzsche phrases it like this: "The will to power can manifest itself only against resistances."[28]

Perhaps other people resist the plans and actions required to achieve the ultimate desire, so you have to make them do what you want. Or perhaps you resist getting up at 4:00 a.m. and putting in all of the extra work, which means you have to make yourself put in the time and effort. Either way, resistance must be overcome, either other people's resistance or your own or both. Knowing that you overcame that resistance, whichever form the resistance takes, breeds feelings of power. Put differently, "the overcoming of resistance is a necessary condition for the satisfaction of the will to power, that is, for *the experience of one's power.*"[29]

Nietzsche's theory of a will to power isn't positive or negative. It's neither socially uplifting nor tyrannical; it encompasses heroes and villains alike. Even though Nietzsche "placed the greatest value on the satisfaction of the feeling of power that comes from self-control or self-mastery or the feeling of capacity, he certainly does not exclude the satisfaction of exerting control over others, of interpersonal domination and of tyranny."[30] As the scholar Ivan Soll puts it, "Self-mastery and the mastery of others are expressions of the same basic drive to power."[31]

Nietzsche makes strong claims about the will to power. Indeed, he claims that "the innermost essence of being is will to power."[32] For Nietzsche, "the basic and innermost thing is still this will."[33] Nietzsche even describes *striving*, as in striving to reach a goal, as "nothing other than striving for power."[34] Nietzsche doesn't specify what one might be striving for, which likely casts a big net around striving—perhaps meaning any kind of striving. It's not hard to see how striving might be considered part of the will to power. But what about the opposite? Take sloth. How does sloth fit into the will to power?

For that matter, does the will to power refer to all behavior, or just some behavior? Does Nietzsche imply that all people work toward their ultimate desires? Many people work hard just to make ends meet, and a privileged few don't appear to have to work at all. So who is aiming to satisfy their ultimate desires? Or is there another way of looking at this seeming conundrum? These questions seem essential if one is to claim, like Nietzsche, that a will to power is the fundamental motivation for all human behavior.

At first glance, such a sweeping claim about human behavior seems fantastic, absurd even. As Soll recognizes, such a monistic motivational theory "may initially strike many of us as implausible."[35] It's hard to exactly link behavior with a specific motivation, especially from the outside. Maybe the apparently spoiled and lazy trust fund twentysomething is aiming toward an ultimate desire no one else can see. Maybe long hours of toil in a seemingly dead-end job are but one of many small steps aimed at an ultimate desire.

In other words, how adjacent, how directly linked and easy-to-see, must a behavior be in connection to an ultimate desire for others to recognize it as such? Further, does it even matter if others can recognize such linkages? Perhaps insisting on an easy-to-see connection between behavior and an ultimate desire only serves to oversimplify Nietzsche's theory. But is an oversimplification the only way to operationalize this theory because gauging the accuracy and verity of Nietzsche's claim is so difficult?

What about everyday behaviors such as going to the kitchen for a glass of milk? Those types of small actions couldn't possibly be aimed toward an ultimate desire. But maybe they don't have to be for Nietzsche's theory to hold. In this light Nietzsche's will to power acts as a sort of heuristic, a promising but fallible hypothesis, that enables economically and cogently exploring the boundaries of motivation. In this light even if the will to power doesn't motivate absolutely all behavior, it might still turn out to be an important aspect of most human action.

4. Action Embedded within Relational Networks

This last line of thinking about power comes from the French philosopher Michel Foucault (1926–1984). Several of Foucault's ideas about power were introduced in chapter 1 and helped create the operational definition of power used in this book—namely, power is not a thing and it cannot be possessed. Power is different from force or coercion; it depends on at least minimal freedom. And power does not act linearly. Instead, it operates more like a web or network. This section will expand on that brief introduction and, perhaps more importantly, will set boundaries on how this book draws from Foucault.

People create power just by being in the world. Foucault claims that power is always exercised with aims and objectives.[36] This denotes choices that are often acted upon other people. These choices are usually embedded within a network of people, perhaps at work, perhaps within one's neighborhood or family. Sometimes, Foucault notes, these choices stem from differences in "economic processes, knowledge relationships, [and] sexual relations."[37] But they are just as likely to involve disagreements over the easement around a driveway.

Foucault's thinking holds some similarities with both Machiavelli and Arendt. Like Machiavelli, Foucault posits power as actions that influence other people's behaviors. Just because power, for Foucault, operates within a network doesn't mean that it doesn't also operate on people or groups. This point can be missed in Foucault's writings, perhaps because he puts so much emphasis on power relations. But what does Foucault mean by a power relation?

Imagine a family or a corporation or a community group, any organization within which people work and/or live together. The members of the group make decisions as they live their lives. Sometimes those decisions change other people's behavior. Say a parent forbids a child to move away for college by implying the removal of approval or financial help. Say a parent gives in to a child's refusal to eat anything but chicken nuggets. Say a younger sister blackmails an older brother by threatening to tell their parents he stole the car last weekend. These are typical, perhaps cliché, examples, but they all illustrate power relations.

These power relations fluctuate. They shift and move as people calculate and act and recalculate and react—not that people are always calculating how to exert power. Rather, people are constantly faced with decisions as they live their lives, and sometimes those decisions involve trying to change other people's behavior. Foucault broadens this analysis to a society-wide scale and, in fact, downplays individual choices. But that analysis, while perhaps useful for an abstract theoretical analysis of societal forces, is difficult to render useful at a life-sized scale. Put differently, it too often ignores the individual.

Unlike Machiavelli, though, and similar to Arendt, Foucault argues that power is not a thing that can be possessed or stored. While Arendt frames her position mostly in terms of language, Foucault bases his argument on the reasoning that because everybody can exert power, nobody can possess power. If power could be possessed, it could be hoarded. It could be taken away, and its use could be limited. But it can't. As long as they possess a modicum of freedom, as long as they are able to resist, even the seemingly lowliest of people can still exert power.

One might object and claim that the ability to exert varying effects of power equates with possessing varying amounts of power. Compare a school superintendent and an elementary student. Superintendents, of course, can exert large-scale effects within a school district, such as hiring and firing staff, creating or deleting programs, and implementing instructional policies. Compared to this, what power can an elementary student exert? They can complete assignments differently than a teacher prescribes. They can choose not to comply with instructions. They can influence how their parents think about the school or the teachers.

These differences in effects are big, and some might claim they result from different amounts of power being held by superintendents as compared to elementary students. For Foucault, however, the net effects of power do not impact whether or not power is a thing. What matters instead is the relationship between the people. Some relations might produce greater differential effects (such as with the superintendent), but this is a result of the nature of the relation, not any power that is supposedly held.

How do these relations form a network, or a web, as this book puts it? Foucault speaks of a network of power relations across society, what he has called "the whole network of the social."[38] This network results from the "possibility of action on the action of others that is coextensive with every social relationship."[39] Put simply, people tend to know lots of other people, and power can be and often is exerted within and across those relationships.

Within a school system, say, a superintendent directs a principal to implement an instructional policy on her campus. The teachers on the campus in turn implement the policy, but they adapt it for their classrooms by deleting parts of the policy and revising others. Students resist the new policy, so the teachers further revise it. Students also complain to their parents about the policy, and the parents complain to the teachers. The principal hears about enough parental complaints that she converses with the superintendent, convincing him to alter the policy. Thus, a network forms from all of these various power exertions.

Not all of Foucault's ideas about power work for this book, though, and it's important to point this out. Unlike the ideas about power from Machiavelli, Arendt, and Nietzsche, it's necessary to cordon off some of Foucault's ideas about power from others. *Power isn't a thing to be possessed; it isn't linear but comes from everywhere and creates a web of power relations.* Those ideas work and align with evidence from schools. Foucault goes further, however, when he positions power alongside truth.

For Foucault, truth isn't something real and objective; it really isn't even subjective. Indeed, he argued that truth doesn't exist except as a product of power. His notion of truth doesn't work for the book. Foucault connects truth and power like this: "Truth is a thing of this world: it is produced only by virtue of multiple forms of constraint."[40] Truth, for Foucault, "is to be understood as a system of ordered procedures for the production, regulation, distribution, circulation, and operation of statements," and thus, it exists only as a "regime," as accepted ways of thinking, being, and acting within "systems of power that produce and sustain it."[41]

What does this mean? It means Foucault believes that power exerted from sources such as society, family, work, and religion shape people's actions and beliefs, thereby making things true or false. Foucault writes extensively about incarceration and the prison system, mental institutions, and sexuality. Within institutions such as these, he claims, power governs not just statements about what is true but also the processes for verifying or falsifying the scientific procedures used to investigate phenomena.

In terms of sexuality, for example, Foucault holds that notions of good and bad regarding practices and feelings are created through power, not from any innate characteristics of the practices or feelings themselves. As Foucault puts it, "The growth of perversions is not a moralizing theme that obsessed the scrupulous minds of the Victorians. It is the real product of the encroachment of a type of power on bodies and their pleasure."[42] In other words, his logic holds that a practice labeled as a perversion, such as, say, pedophilia, is only a perversion because of restrictions caused by power, not by anything inherently wrong with pedophilia.

Foucault applies his theories broadly across society and phenomena. Indeed, Foucault connects his truth/power claims all the way down to individual people when he asserts that "power had to be able to gain access to the bodies of individuals, to their acts, attitudes, and modes of everyday behavior."[43] Since he places no limits on his "truth is not real but is only created by power" arguments, one might ask, Is the school down the street not truly a school? Is a star not truly a star? Does water not freeze and become ice? Or are all of those statements merely guided by power?

These truth/power claims are a bridge too far. They don't withstand close scrutiny. Take the claim that smoking is bad for your health. Is this claim created and enforced merely by powerful interests, as if companies made money off people *not* smoking? Of course not. It's supported by mountains of scientific, medical, and experiential evidence. What about Jean Piaget's claim that people usually learn to do concrete tasks before more abstract ones? The answer is no again. People usually learn, say, simple addition before they learn to play chess. Might exceptions to these claims exist? Perhaps, but they would be supported with empirical evidence.

Can this book use some of Foucault's ideas about power but not others? Can it pick and choose only the most useful, most relevant ideas and discard the others? Of course. Ideas don't come in bundles. If you hire a decorator to redesign your house, can you agree with the bathroom tile selections but reject the ideas for the tile in the living room? Certainly, and not just because it's your house. Some ideas work well together, and others don't. Some ideas fit the circumstances, and others don't. Using some but not all of Foucault's ideas about power does not weaken the ideas selected. What matters most is how well they contribute to understanding.

WHY FOUCAULT AND NOT MACHIAVELLI, ARENDT, OR NIETZSCHE?

One can ask the same question in comparison with the other thinkers. Why use ideas from Foucault to analyze how power works in schools and not ideas from Machiavelli, Arendt, Nietzsche, or the other thinkers? In short, because they fit the evidence better. The ideas from Machiavelli, Arendt, and Nietzsche each hold appeal in different ways. Schools can feel like cutthroat places (Machiavelli). Educators do occasionally come together in free agreement to generate new ideas (Arendt). And many teachers do seem to work from a type of calling (Nietzsche). But none of those three captures real-life dynamics quite like Foucault's ideas do.

Start with Machiavelli. Power in schools certainly does change other people's behaviors. It happens daily. Indeed, it's supposed to happen. Schools, like any large organization, would be nigh impossible to run if leaders didn't give directions and subordinates didn't follow them. Principals need to run schools, and teachers need to run classrooms. And most educators feel the pressures of accountability ratings and mandated testing. So at first response, it seems like Machiavelli's thinking about power might align with the realities of schooling.

However, nobody gains and holds power at any cost. The ends do not justify the means, and in schools, the means matter. Further, educators share power in schools; they don't consolidate it. Superintendents, principals, teachers, and other staff all play roles and all exert power in different ways. There is no prince. While some educators might connive and play power games, most do not. Most collaborate, however imperfectly. Teachers usually plan together as teams. The best administrators value input from their staff. Even superintendents meet with advisory boards and listen to their principals.

Superintendents and principals can, of course, micromanage and run roughshod over the educators they supervise, bending them to their will. But this is usually a mistake in the long run. Superintendents and principals don't possess all of the information, so they don't know all of the answers. Plus, they are distant from students, at least as compared to teachers. They can spend loads of time with teachers and students inside classrooms, and they can gain a deep understanding of the teaching and learning going on there.

But it's not the superintendent or principal doing the teaching. So superintendents and principals can know a lot, but they're always removed from those teaching and learning relationships. Thus, they rely—or at least they should rely—on the judgment and expertise of their staff. This is a difficult dance. Principals in particular are responsible for students' learning outcomes in their schools. And they have an obligation to direct and guide teachers to help them achieve those outcomes, leading them up or out, as a common saying goes.

Sometimes principals are the "principal teacher" in a school,[44] the head teacher who administers through the authority, not of the position but of the quality and nature of her teaching expertise and her ability to develop her teachers, in order to "move them up." Yet sometimes principals must lead teachers out of their campus. Because of their position, they can let teachers go (even if the process can be long and difficult). They could just operate by imposing power. But the risk is getting it wrong; thus, principals are cautioned against wanton use of power.

This is another reason Machiavelli's principles don't really work in schools. The prince had all the information; principals don't, and there's no way they can get it. The prince didn't rely on others; principals rely on lots of people to do their jobs well. The prince could manipulate others; that doesn't work too well on teachers. The prince could punish others; that never works well on a staff. The prince could bribe others; that only works if you want to go to jail. In short, the contexts and purposes of school don't allow power manipulation at any cost. Machiavelli's ideas about power, then, might work narrowly, but they don't work for the whole of schools.

What about Arendt? Educators seem to share a common motivation, what Arendt calls a *common will*. If asked why they teach, most teachers would likely answer something to the effect of they do it for the students. While the benefits can be good and the schedule can be nice (Who doesn't enjoy two weeks off at Christmas?), most teachers—all educators, for that matter—don't do the job just for the perks. Most value the experience of teaching, the learning and mentoring relationships with students, giving to the community, or other similar reasons.

So one might think that a common will needs little help to be formed. And from what one might call a "low-resolution" point of view, that's true. But as they say, the devil is in the details. Everyone wants what's best for students, but few people agree on what *best* means—or on how to get there. Sometimes disagreements arise simply over the style, format, or method that teaching will take, say, between a more lecture-oriented approach and a more question-oriented approach. In that case, disagreements about what is best might refer to the kinds of cognitive processes that teachers expect from students.

Disagreements often relate to the burden imposed by standardized accountability testing. Achieving high scores always matters to school boards and school administrators; indeed, their job security often directly relates to it. But how to achieve high scores often creates tensions. Many times, decisions about how to pursue high scores are imposed onto teachers, who then feel forced to change sometimes long-standing teaching practices. For example, researcher Cheryl Craig details how one school reform effort turned how a middle school literacy teacher felt about her work as a teacher from one as curriculum developer to curriculum implementer.[45]

In that case, the nonprofit organization supporting the reform effort, the staff developer hired to implement the reform, and the literacy teacher all felt like they were working toward the students' best interests. What resulted, however, was an experienced and effective teacher feeling like she was a "butterfly under a pin."[46] These types of examples are unfortunately common, as school systems grapple with the best way to achieve high test scores. A "high-resolution" inquiry into teaching, then, shows that educators seldom form a detailed common will.

Nor can educators easily engage in the type of free conversations that Arendt finds essential. Well, they can—but only behind closed doors. Free conversations will necessarily produce dissenting views, but once teachers and principals share dissenting views publicly, they take risks. The researchers Michael Connelly and Jean Clandinin frame this dilemma as between "stories of school" and "school stories."[47]

A "story of school" is a story told *about* a school, usually by policymakers, perhaps by a local chamber of commerce, or maybe by a superintendent or a school board. A story of school often tries to burnish a school's public image by reinforcing sacrosanct messaging about the school. A "school story," on the other hand, is a story told on the inside by educators as they talk openly amongst themselves. School stories contain unvarnished beliefs—sometimes critical, sometimes supportive—that educators share with each other related to their experiences within the system.

Teachers and principals live in the tension between these two types of stories, frequently crossing the boundaries between them. One is a safe space for free conversation; the other isn't. This dynamic circumscribes the horizon of possible activity that educators might have. Teachers' horizons are limited. They must always negotiate obstacles, sometimes avoiding them, sometimes accommodating them, and other times submitting to them. Put simply, they never get to see or really even imagine an unrestricted possibility. For all of these reasons, Arendt's theories about power don't work for analyzing how it operates in schools.

How about Nietzsche, then? Like Machiavelli and Arendt, Nietzsche's theory about power also seems applicable to schools, at least at first glance. If most teachers teach for the students, then they seem intrinsically drawn to teaching. One might say that through teaching, many teachers experience their own power and that teaching is a way for teachers to operationalize their power. This seems to align with Nietzsche's notion of a will to power. Plus, Nietzsche holds that a will to power only manifests against resistance. Teaching, then, seems to fulfill these two requirements: teachers work for the kids, and they always face resistance in their work.

However, two big problems exist with using Nietzsche's will to power to analyze power in schools. First, nobody can actually know if teachers experience a will to power through teaching. A will to power enacts one's ultimate desire, and these ultimate desires hold value for people for their own sake. Within schools this would mean that teachers teach and principals lead for no other reason than because those pursuits hold intrinsic value. The problem is that just because most educators likely work for the students, this doesn't mean that's their ultimate desire.

Maybe the high school English teacher really cares about kids but actually wants to write novels and is figuring out how to get started again in writing after life circumstances veered her into teaching. Maybe the music or art teacher actually wanted to perform or create, but he just wasn't talented enough, so he teaches instead. Maybe the middle school math teacher never had a grand plan. She liked math well enough in college to major in it but found she had no career direction upon graduating, so she wandered into teaching. All of these teachers, though, care about kids and try to help them, even if they deep down might prefer to do other work.

The second problem is that the notion of a will to power doesn't seem to apply to the variety of ways that power manifests in schools. Here, of course, two different conceptions of power collide: power as will and power as force or influence. In schools people tell other people what to do. That isn't bad. Schools need organization. That order giving could be part of people's will to power. But as was just argued above, there's no way to know people's innermost motivation for working in schools. This makes it likely that order giving as a part of running schools comes not from a will to power but from just trying to get things done.

Further, people can exert influence in subtle ways in schools. Take the example of teachers changing a scope and sequence. School districts often prescribe the pace, sequence, and range of curriculum to be taught. Experienced teachers, however, often change those plans to fit their particular classes, students, or knowledge of teaching. Thus, teachers may exert influence—or power—over this crucial aspect of their teaching. This could connect to one's ultimate desire. But it could also, as with order giving, result from just trying to make a class run more effectively (and be without any deeper motivation).

Nietzsche's will to power, in short, isn't nuanced enough to theorize power in schools, and it fails to account for too many subtle actions in schools. Schools aren't designed to accommodate individuality. Individual preference exists but only in the margins. Those margins are crucial, of course (arranging lessons, conducting formative assessment, selecting books, relating to students, and more), but they do not connect to the larger institutional structures in schools. Nor does a will to power reflect the subtleties of teaching or the moral aspects of teaching, which is what scholar David Hansen calls the "poetics of teaching."[48]

Of these four ways of thinking about power, then, the selected ideas from Foucault best describe how power works in schools (not all of Foucault's notions about power, mind you). Truth exists in schools, and it isn't all connected to power. Some ways of working with most students work better than others. Some forms of assessment stimulate learning more effectively than others. Some strategies for leading class discussions develop higher-order thinking more successfully than others. Only those more limited theories work well for schools.

These particular claims from Foucault fill in the gaps the other philosophers leave. For example, unlike Nietzsche's will to power, Foucault's thinking covers both overt and subtle exertions of power. Power comes from big school reform efforts, such as statewide curriculum and testing changes. But it also comes from teachers and students inside the confines of classrooms, which is difficult to see unless you are there in classrooms with teachers.

Like with Arendt, power cannot be possessed. But unlike Arendt's theory, power is not dependent on free conversation, which is helpful since so little conversation in schools is truly unrestricted. Like with Machiavelli, teachers should be mindful of power coming from unexpected sources and should plan as best they can to address competing power claims to try to mitigate the impact on students' learning. Unlike Machiavelli's theory, power isn't a zero-sum game, and the ends don't justify the means. Power is always shared in schools since it can't be possessed, and schools rely on effective power distribution.

NOTES

1. Julie Battilana and Tiziana Casciaro, *Power for all: How it really works and why it's everyone's business* (New York: Simon & Schuster, 2021), x.
2. Mihaly Csikszentmihaly, *The evolving self: A psychology for the third millennium* (New York: Harper Perennial, 1993), 89.
3. Jurgen Habermas and Thomas McCarthy, "Hannah Arendt's communications concept of power," *Social Research* 44, no. 1 (Spring 1977): 3.
4. Max Weber, *Economy and society*, trans. Guenther Roth and Claus Wittich (Berkeley, CA: University of California Press, 1978).
5. Talcott Parsons, "On the concept of political power," in *Politics and social structure*, ed. Talcott Parsons (New York: Free Press, 1969), 353.
6. Bertrand Russell, *Power* (London: Routledge Classics, 2004), 6.
7. Russell, *Power*, 6.
8. Russell, *Power*, 13.
9. Niccolo Machiavelli, *The prince*, trans. George Bull (London: Penguin Classics, 2003).
10. Machiavelli, *The prince*, 82.
11. Oxford Reference, "Machiavellian," accessed on June 17, 2023 from https://www.oxfordreference.com/display/10.1093/acref/9780198609810.001.0001/acref-9780198609810-e-4250
12. Machiavelli, *The prince*, 53.
13. Machiavelli, *The prince*, 56.
14. Machiavelli, *The prince*, 72.
15. Machiavelli, *The prince*, 29.
16. Machiavelli, *The prince*, 11.
17. Talcott Parsons, *Structure and process in modern societies* (Glencoe, IL: Free Press, 1960), 181.
18. Hannah Arendt, *On violence* (New York: Harcourt, Brace & World, 1970), 44.
19. Leo J. Penta, "Hannah Arendt: On power," *The Journal of Speculative Philosophy* 10, no. 3 (1996): 212.
20. Penta, "Hannah Arendt: On power," 214.
21. Csikszentmihaly, *The evolving self*, 89.
22. Habermas and McCarthy, "Hannah Arendt's communications," 6.
23. Penta, "Hannah Arendt: On power," 212.
24. Parsons, "On the concept of political power," 232.
25. Friedrich Nietzsche, *The will to power*, trans. Walter Kaufmann and R. J. Hollingdale, ed. Walter Kaufmann (New York: Vintage Books, 1967), 366.
26. Ivan Soll, "Nietzsche disempowered: Reading the will to power out of Nietzsche's philosophy," *Journal of Nietzsche Studies* 46, no. 3 (Autumn 2015): 426.
27. Ivan Soll, "Nietzsche's will to power as a psychological thesis," *Journal of Nietzsche Studies* 43, no. 1 (Spring 2012): 125.
28. Nietzsche, *The will to power*, 346.
29. Soll, "Nietzsche's will to power," 123; emphasis in the original.
30. Soll, "Nietzsche's will to power," 123.

31. Soll, "Nietzsche's will to power," 123.
32. Nietzsche, *The will to power*, 369.
33. Nietzsche, *The will to power*, 368.
34. Nietzsche, *The will to power*, 368.
35. Soll, "Nietzsche disempowered," 442.
36. Helmut Staubmann, "C. Wright Mills' The sociological imagination and the construction of Talcott Parsons as a conservative grand theorist," *The American Sociologist* 52 (March 2021): 187.
37. Michel Foucault, *The history of sexuality: An introduction. Volume I*, trans. Robert Hurley (New York: Vintage Books, 1990), 94.
38. Michel Foucault, *Power*, ed. James D. Faubion (New York: The New Press, 2000), 345.
39. Foucault, *Power*, 345.
40. Foucault, *Power*, 131.
41. Foucault, *Power*, 132.
42. Foucault, *The history of sexuality*, 48.
43. Foucault, *Power*, 125.
44. This notion of "principal teacher" is drawn from Ted Aoki, "Beyond the half-life of curriculum and pedagogy," *One world* 27, no. 2 (1990).
45. Cheryl J. Craig, "'Butterfly under a pin': An emergent teacher image amid mandated curriculum reform," *Journal of Educational Research* 105, no. 2 (February 2012): 90–101.
46. Craig, "'Butterfly under a pin,'" 90–101.
47. Clandinin and Connelly, "Teachers' professional knowledge landscapes: Teacher stories," 24–30.
48. David T. Hansen, "A poetics of teaching," *Educational Theory* 54, no. 2 (April 2004): 119–42.

Chapter 3

Students' Power to Define Themselves

Chapter 3 looks at the first part of the definition of power: power is not a thing. What does it mean to say that power is not a thing? It means that power cannot be stored, nor can it be withheld. If power can't be withheld, that means that all manner of people might exert power, even in the most unlikely and hard-to-see ways, even by people who might commonly be considered as powerless. This book's practical examination of power begins in one of these unlikely places—with students.

However, it doesn't begin with anything obvious, like walkouts or sit-ins. Actions like that have been well covered, and they're overtly political, so thinking about them and responses to them must also be political. Plus, they're rare, at least in any one particular school. In fact, most schools never experience public political protests like walkouts. If they do happen, of course, these political actions cause serious disruptions, as well as spotlight the issues being protested.[1] But the effects are usually only temporary; everybody goes home, and the day-to-day business of schooling quickly resumes.

Instead of looking at more sensational things, then, this chapter starts small and subtle and looks at power that emerges within the daily routines of schooling . . . and that might even be masked by those daily routines. Specifically, the chapter claims that students possess power that few people see—the manner in which "gifted and talented" (GT) students define themselves as GT. This phenomenon illustrates how power is not a thing.

How is this an example of power *not* being a thing? The answer is because it shows that neither schools, teachers, nor researchers solely possess the power to define kids. And it's not that both schools *and* students possess the power to define students: it's that *neither* possesses power, but both can *exert* power. As this chapter will show, this particular power of students "hid" in plain sight, so to speak, right under teachers,' principals,' and even researchers' noses.

It likely hid because nobody thought of it as power and because the conditions necessary for it to reveal itself seldom occur in classrooms and schools. This begs another question: Does power have to be seen for it to exist? Or, put differently, can power exist even if nobody knows about it or sees its actions? According to this book's operational definition of power, the answer must be yes. Power need not be easily visible to exert influence.

This is the case with students' power to define themselves. Students get defined and described in schools in a wide variety of ways. Some definitions might be said to come to school with the students. For example, no school committee meets to determine a student's ethnicity. Many students, of course, have had to work hard to exert power over their expression of personal characteristics. But students bring these qualities with them to school—no one at school assigns them to students.

Other definitions and descriptions *do* get assigned to students by schools. There are lots of them, such as English language learner, 504, emotionally disturbed, at-risk, and more. Students don't claim these labels for themselves; educators determine them and apply them to students. Unlike, say, their ethnicity, students do not get to select their at-risk status, their English language learner status, or any of the other educational labels; they just receive the label.

It's easy and likely common to think that students are powerless against these labels, especially the younger that the students are. You may ask, how could they exert power when everything seems so imposed onto them? Yet the truth is students can and do exert power over the substance and meaning of these kinds of educational labels, just not the kind of power one might expect. In fact, this power is easy to miss—most educators and researchers miss it.

This chapter tells the story of how middle school students in two eighth-grade US history classes exerted power over the meaning of their GT label.[2] These students' power was meaningful but extremely subtle. Their teachers, Margaret Rhodes and Bill Trammell, never saw their power. The students themselves never recognized their power. Indeed, it took almost an entire school year for anyone, including this author, to recognize their power. But that power holds ramifications for educational research into giftedness and for the design of gifted programs. It demonstrates how even a subtle power can hold potentially pernicious effects.

WHAT IS A GT LABEL?

School systems routinely evaluate students for "giftedness" and then implement programs or plans of action to try to meet those students' learning needs.

These students often receive a gifted and talented, or GT, label that signals to the students and to the students' family, friends, and teachers that the students require different educational services than do "regular," or non-GT, students. Sometimes, such as in the classrooms researched for this study, GT students are separated into special classes for only GT students. In this case, students were separated into a special US history class for GT students.

Like other labels in schools, the meaning of the GT label is determined for students and affixed onto them by a committee of school personnel. Students just need to qualify depending on the criteria used by the school district.[3] Definitions of giftedness are created by education researchers. These definitions have changed over the years from an initial focus on just cognitive ability toward a broader inclusion of creativity and perseverance.[4] Scholars work out these definitions through research articles published in academic journals, and the definitions filter down to school districts and school programs.

Here power is clearly at work: the power exerted by scholars and school personnel to create and impose models and definitions of giftedness onto students that will substantially shape their educational experiences. These definitions shape classroom discourse. Spend time in any GT classroom in any public school in the country, and you'll most likely hear a similar discourse. On the surface it'll appear that the teachers and students all share the same understanding of what GT means, a sort of tacitly but commonly held understanding of giftedness.

This is because the teacher sets the terms of the conversation. The teacher talks to students about what "being GT" means, and the students go along with it. At no time will the teacher and students hash out together in class what giftedness or GT means. Nor will the teacher ask students what they think giftedness or GT means. Students' lack of input creates a contradiction. As one researcher puts it, "Children themselves are, paradoxically, often absent from the current models and theories of giftedness," even though the "subjective perspective seems to be vital to understanding the development of . . . high-achieving children."[5]

ESTABLISHING CONTEXT: A BRIEF REVIEW OF THE RESEARCH LITERATURE

At least since the 1950s, education researchers have been trying to understand gifted students' perceptions of labels of giftedness. Students' perceptions of their GT labels are important because the label can cause children to perceive themselves differently.[6] Researchers claim that GT students' perceptions of the label can influence their academic achievement, as well as their social and emotional development.[7] Researchers have found mixed responses from students about the label: some studies have found positive perceptions of the GT label, while other studies have found more negative reactions to the label.

Many studies find that gifted students hold positive views of their abilities.[8] In a study with 184 GT high school students, 64 percent of students saw giftedness as performance, and 36 percent viewed it as a trait, with 79 percent of all students viewing the label positively.[9] A different study, this time with 365 middle school students, reports that a positive relationship exists between gifted students' implicit beliefs about giftedness and intelligence.[10] Another study of 295 GT students reports that students "believe that giftedness can be attained by hard work and that gifted and talented students are not very different from other [students]."[11]

Other researchers, however, have found less positive results. For example, a study of 85 seventh-, eighth-, and ninth-grade students reports that even though students' "associations to their experience of giftedness seemed largely positive," 80 percent of the students were unable to take strong ownership of their giftedness: "only 20 [percent] of the students responded to the 'I consider myself gifted' item in either the 'very much' or 'extremely' category."[12] Indeed, parents, teachers, and friends were much more likely to identify students as gifted than students were to self-identify as gifted.[13]

Additionally, research focusing on adolescents' emotional struggles with labels of giftedness illustrates how students, in contrast to the positive associations described above, can sometimes also go to great lengths to avoid or downplay giftedness labels.[14] The researchers contend that "many children who are gifted experience being gifted as if it were a stigma," and they claim that "if given a chance to call attention to their differentness (giftedness)," gifted students will often choose "to soften the sharpness of the difference."[15] One student was quoted, saying, "Being one of the smarties isn't easy. It's a social handicap and everyone stares."[16]

RESEARCHING STUDENTS' PERCEPTIONS OF THE GT LABEL

The study on which this chapter is based examined students' perceptions of the GT label and how they defined themselves as GT.[17] When researchers study GT students' perceptions of their GT label, they usually use instruments such as Likert scales or open-ended questionnaires to measure students' thoughts, feelings, and perceptions.[18] While those research methods can produce useful information, they are nonetheless limited. In using those research instruments, regardless of how open-ended or comprehensive those questionnaires might be, researchers only capture a single response or a single collection of responses regarding students' thinking.

In contrast to those typical research methods, this study hoped to discover what would happen if researchers gave students the time, freedom, and opportunity to talk at length in extended conversations about their perceptions of and experiences with the GT label. What would students say? Would their thinking and descriptions remain consistent? Or would they contradict themselves? Further, how might this speak to the ways in which research on GT students' perceptions of their giftedness labels is conducted?[19]

What the Findings Revealed

The research literature on students' perceptions of the GT label makes two major claims: (1) that GT students either accept *or* reject the label, and (2) that students hold either a volitional or an intrinsic interpretation of the label. The literature does not make allowances for gray areas in which students hold conflicting views of the label—for students simultaneously accepting *and* rejecting the label—nor for students holding both volitional *and* intrinsic interpretations of it. Instead, that literature portrays students as holding firm and uncomplicated beliefs about their GT label.

The findings from this study, however, contradict all of that. The findings reveal that students could, at the same time, both accept and reject their GT label, and they could hold both a volitional and an intrinsic view of the label. Further, this study illustrates how GT classes can become a world within a world in which GT students isolate from non-GT or "regular" students and even impute personal characteristics to non-GT students.

Accepting and Rejecting the GT Label

The giftedness literature implies that students *either* accept or reject the label. This study, however, suggests that these students *both* accept and reject the label at the same time. For example, students claimed to be more motivated and more interested in learning than non-GT students but, at the same time, no different from non-GT students. During an interview, one of their teachers, Bill Trammell, tried to explain this phenomenon. This excerpt picks up after Bill learned about the "We're not geniuses" comment one student made: "They do want to have it both ways. It's something because there is this culture of being apart and being on a pedestal in some ways. They like certain aspects of that, when it's to their advantage. But as soon as it becomes a hindrance in any way, they're going to back on that, saying, 'It doesn't mean we're geniuses!'"

The following statements from students show them distancing themselves from the label:

- "We're not really different from, like, from the regular class. Like our work is a little more difficult in detail, like the tests that they give us and the worksheets that they give us . . . [a pause] but it's not, we're not any smarter than them or anything."
- "I hate—I don't like the fact that they think just because we're GT, we're more capable or, like, or we're smarter."
- "Yeah, it gets to us cause, like, people think because we're GT, we're so different."
- "We're not geniuses. I mean, we're not Albert Einstein."
- "It just bothers me when people tell me that cause I don't see the difference between a regular student and a GT student. It's just because of a test we took way back."

In these statements, the students tried to draw closer to "regular" students by arguing how they really were not that different from non-GT students.

Other statements, however, show the same students embracing the label. In this embracing of the label, however, students seemed to position non-GT students as "other" and arguably lesser beings. These statements implied a tacit corollary, which is noted in brackets after each statement (note that students' use of the pronoun "they" refers to non-GT students):

- "They don't really have an interest to learn, really." [We do have an interest to learn.]
- "They're just there because they have to be." [We are there because we want to be.]
- "Like regular classes, like, they'll pretty much just do the main points." [We do more than the main points.]
- "Like it would get kind of boring." [We want our learning to be engaging.]
- "They just cover the basic stuff." [We cover more than the basic stuff.]
- "They don't like going into depth." [We like going into depth.]
- "Like, for us, it wouldn't really suffice." [Because we want more from our lessons.]

These examples illustrate how students denied one difference (being smarter than non-GT students) while, at the same time, embracing other differences (that they saw things in a different way and were more interested in learning).

This vacillation between different interpretations of the GT label and between accepting and rejecting the label seems, in some ways, to align with findings in giftedness researcher Laurence Coleman's work regarding adolescents' difficulty in accepting their GT label.[20] That work found that adolescents often identified GT labels as a stigma and would frequently try to downplay their giftedness.

Similarly, the students in this study downplayed their intelligence as compared to non-GT students, even though they clearly outscored "regular" students across a variety of measures. None of their discourse, however, suggests that these students found the label to be a stigma. Some students' discourse implies that they grew weary of spending most of the school day with the same people. But none of the discourse states or implies that students found the GT label to be socially burdensome.

Volitional and Intrinsic Interpretations of GT

The students in this study told a number of different narratives about what the GT label meant to them. Some of these narratives seem to reflect previous findings about GT students' perceptions of the GT label: some reflect a volitional, or choice, interpretation of GT; others reflect an intrinsic, or trait, interpretation of GT.[21] Yet other discourse compounds these qualities into broader and messier definitions that seem to simultaneously reflect both interpretations of GT. Further, two students even made the claim for there being no differences at all between GT and non-GT students.

The "Volitional" Interpretation

The volitional interpretation implies that GT was a sort of club which, as long as they met the entrance requirements, students could choose whether or not to join. Intelligence seemed to be taken for granted here; what mattered was if a student was willing to participate in differentiated instruction (i.e., was willing to practice being a GT student). This narrative maintains that GT and non-GT students were usually equally smart but that GT students simply chose to do the extra schoolwork required in GT classes. In the following passage, one student cogently described this interpretation: "Some of the kids, they can't be in GT. They don't like doing the homework, but they're still really smart. But they just don't like having to do the homework, yeah, like having to do the homework and stuff like that. So they just take regular classes so it won't be too much."

Usually the students did not directly state this interpretation, but rather implied it in their discourse. In the following transcript excerpt, for example, notice how one student referred to a reason why students "joined" GT:

Author: Is that just a bunch of extra work?

Student 1: It was more work.

Student 2: That's a part of GT. That's why we joined.

Student 3: It's not like regular, mainstream classes.

Student 4: It's like we usually go, like, more . . .

Student 2: We usually get, like, more projects.

Author: Deeper into it?

Student 4: Yeah.

Student 2's statement "That's why we joined" implied a choice of whether or not to be GT. Students 2 and 4 hinted that one reason they chose to join GT was for the extra projects and opportunities for going deeper into class curriculum.

Some students combined a volitional interpretation with an attribution of different values. In the excerpt below, students first argued that there is little difference between GT and non-GT students but then attributed to the two groups differences in work ethic and desire to learn:

Author: So, y'all said that, that there are no differences. But then you said, wait a minute, kids who are not in GT classes are not as open to learning. They're lazier.

Student: Oh, no, we're not saying, cause not all of them. We kinda like stereotyped them, but it's just like if we want to be more, if we kinda want to get more advanced in, like, like, or more like into depth into a subject.

At times students expressed difficulty in embracing their "choice" to be GT. For example, the excerpt below shows several students reinforcing to themselves that their choice will eventually be "worth it":

Author: Is it worth it?

Students: [A large collective breath]

Student 1: Yeah, you understand more, and I guess—

Author: You say yeah, but I see two shrugs.

Student 2: It's not like—

Student 3: Well, it's not like we have a choice.

Student 1: Well, we do have a choice . . .

Student 2: It'll be worth it.

Student 1: . . . we could stop.

Student 3: It'll be worth it in the end.

In this excerpt, students justified their decision to "be GT." Student 3 implied that his or her choice was made for him or her. Even though only Student 1 directly stated that he or she had a choice of whether to continue or stop, all of the justifications implied collective agreement that they were choosing to be GT.

The "Intrinsic" Interpretation

The intrinsic interpretation, on the other hand, refers to an ontological quality in students, something students carried around with them between their ears.[22] Similar to students who articulated volitional interpretations of GT, students who expressed an intrinsic interpretation clearly rejected any notion that they were smarter than non-GT students and instead accounted for their GT label by claiming that they simply saw things in a "different way."

Instead of intelligence, students emphasized perception as the defining characteristic of giftedness.[23] The following exchange is a representative example of this argument:

Student: I hate—I don't like the fact that they think just because we're GT we're more capable or, like, or we're smarter.

Author: Isn't that—

Student: It's more like we're just gifted. We see things in a different way.

Other students expressed equal passion in deflecting the notion of superior intelligence and claiming a difference in perception:

Student 1: But like, yeah, that would be easy, but then again, we're still in eighth grade, so we don't really know much.

Author: But you're GT.

Student 1: Yeah, but—

Student 2: GT doesn't necessarily . . . why does everybody say that?

Student 3: Yeah, it gets to us cause, like, people think because we're GT, we're so different.

Student 2: We're not geniuses. I mean, we're not Albert Einstein.

Student 1: They just give us more work, that's basically . . .

Student 2: We're not.

Student 1: ... the difference.

Student 3: They give us more homework and harder tests.

Student 2: It just means that you understand things at a higher level.

Here is an example of how closely these different interpretations of GT coexisted within students' discourse. The author's comment "But you're GT" was intended to provoke a response from students. Immediately, they rejected both the notion of them being smarter than non-GT students and of them being "so different." Students 1 and 3 seemed to offer a volitional interpretation of GT in that GT students were willing to accept "more homework and harder tests." Then student 2 stated the intrinsic interpretation that GT students "understand things at a higher level."

Both Interpretations at the Same Time

The giftedness literature describes students as holding clearly defined perceptions of giftedness labels. However, in this study, clear boundaries did not exist between the different interpretations of the label, because students' discourse did not consistently adhere to just one of the interpretations—that is, students' discourse over the course of the interviews would, at times, imply that they held multiple interpretations.

For example, in one group interview, the following discourse implies a volitional interpretation of GT:

Student 3: Well, it's not like we have a choice.

Student 1: Well, we do have a choice ...

Student 2: It'll be worth it.

Student 1: ... we could stop.

Student 3: It'll be worth it in the end.

Students talked about having a choice, that they could stop being GT, and that it would be "worth it in the end" to continue being GT. All of these statements imply that students thought being GT was a choice they could make.

However, in that same interview, another sample of discourse from the same group of students implies an intrinsic interpretation of GT:

Author: Wait, what's a GT extension?

Student 1: You get extra questions.

Student 3: It's only for the GT class.

Student 4: And they count against us; it's not like for extra credit.

Author: So it's added on.

Student 2: Yeah, the GT part of the test.

Student 1: It's an extra part of the test.

Student 3: Cause we're expected to know more.

Student 1: And we're expected to be more advanced.

Students 3 and 1 voiced an intrinsic interpretation when they claimed, respectively, "Cause we're expected to know more" and "We're expected to be more advanced."

It is possible, of course, that these students were in fact expressing a volitional interpretation: students could have been expected to know more because they chose to participate in GT classes. Elsewhere in this particular interview with these students, they expressed other comments about GT that were classified as indicating a volitional interpretation. However, these particular statements seem to convey an intrinsic interpretation through the students' tone of voice, which signaled pressure from teachers not from a choice to join GT but just because the students *were* GT.

No Difference at All

The smallest (but still important) claim students made was that no differences at all existed between GT and non-GT students. One student passionately said the following: "I'll talk louder. Like not rebelling, I don't like being disrespectful, but it just bothers me when people tell me that cause I don't see the difference between a regular student and a GT student. It's just because of a test we took way back."

Another student more calmly explained that the GT students and non-GT students were the same: "GT is just, it stands for gifted and talented, but we're not really different from, like, from the regular class. Like our work is a little more difficult in detail, like the tests that they give us and the worksheets that they give us . . . [a pause] but it's not, we're not any smarter than them or anything. We just get a little bit more difficult work. That's it."

For the first student, the differences in scores on "a test [they] took way back" did not equal more substantive differences between students with and without the GT label. For the second student, GT students simply received different work but were no smarter than non-GT students.

A World within a World

Related to the different interpretations of the GT label was the students' emphasis on being different from non-GT students. This difference was often central to the narratives that students told about GT. These differences were oftentimes articulated in value-laden terms. The two teachers clearly articulated to students during classes that "more" was expected of them because they were GT. Here are several statements Margaret Rhodes, the other teacher in the study, made one day while describing the requirements for a project:

- "Remember, your quiz is different. You have to write what it means to you."
- "That's part of being, the GT part of this."
- "Remember, you are GT. More is expected."
- "It has to be a level above. Otherwise, you can go back to regular classes."

During interviews students reiterated Margaret's emphasis on differentiation from non-GT classes. For example, in the transcript excerpt below, students highlighted that a GT student's work must be "more" than a "regular" student's work. This short excerpt picks up from a conversation about projects given to students over various holidays:

Student 1: Yeah, well, like you're gonna be with family and stuff like that, and it's the kind of project that you wanted to put a lot into. Cause she [Ms. Rhodes] would emphasize because, like, we're in GT like.

Student 2: It has to be more than like a regular student's project, or something we have to put, like, more time into it.

This emphasis on performance especially applied to accountability exams. Bill explained the difference: "Yeah, that was right before [the state mandated standardized exam]. Everybody was given a goal in GT of getting commended, so that's what I was expecting of them." For that particular exam, "commended" represented a substantially higher score than an "acceptable" rating. Margaret also stressed this test performance expectation. In one instance she told the GT class, "In here, your goal is to get commended. It should be 100 percent commended in here." In a later exchange with a student that same period, Margaret clarified the student's understanding of the expectations:

Margaret: Fifty percent of you got commended.

Student: Isn't that a lot?

Margaret: Not for GT. My GT classes get 90–100 percent commended.

Students similarly described the difference between GT and non-GT classes in terms of extra work assigned to GT classes that was not assigned to non-GT classes:

Author: So the test is harder for GT?

Student 1: Even the projects sometimes.

Student 2: He [Mr. Trammell] gives us projects sometimes that the other kids don't have to do.

Student 3: We got a project that the other kids don't get.

Student 4: Or like the inventions project. We had to choose, like . . .

Student 5: Extra.

Student 4: . . . it was eleven, well we had to choose three more. We had to do all the extra work.

Student 2: It was seven and we had to do nine.

Student 4: And there was, like, four extra credit, and they could do it for extra credit, but we had to do two out of those extra credit.

Student 1: It wasn't for extra credit; we had to.

Within this emphasis on difference, students made references to in-groups and out-groups. For example, notice Student 4's claim that "we had to do two out of the extra credit" but "they could do it for extra credit." "We," of course, refers to GT students, and "they" refers to non-GT students. In another example, students in the transcript below offered more specific allusions to differences in worlding:

Author: I hear this GT thing a lot. What is GT?

Student 1: Gifted and talented. Basically, it means you take, um, honors classes or whatever.

Student 2: They'll give you more work than a regular student, and they expect more from you.

Student 3: It's like higher advanced than the regular peoples.

Student 3's phrase "the regular peoples" seems to imply a group of people who are substantively different from what students in other focus groups called GT people.

Sometimes students not only framed differences between GT and non-GT classes in terms of differences between "us" and "them," but they also attributed value differences to the two groups. In the exchange below, students referred to depth and complexity in classroom content but also claimed that "they" (meaning non-GT students) did not have the same preference for depth in learning that GT students held:

Student 1: Like that's what GT's for.

Author: To go into more depth [students had introduced the word "depth" earlier in the conversation].

Student 1: Yeah.

Student 2: Yeah.

Student 3: And more like in depth, like regular classes, like they'll pretty much just do the main points.

Student 2: Like it would get kind of boring.

Student 1: They just cover the basic stuff.

Student 3: Yeah.

Student 2: They don't like going into depth.

Student 1: Like for us, it wouldn't really suffice, cause it's just—

Student 3: We like to ask questions.

In this example, students made explicit distinctions in discourse between self and other: "we" like asking questions, but "they" don't; "we" would get bored with the basic stuff, but for "them," it suffices. In this same focus group interview, students went so far as to directly claim that non-GT students had a lower desire to learn than GT students.

Student 1: The class just goes smoother.

Student 2: We'll, like, get little extras.

Author: So, do you feel like the teachers treat GT classes differently? Do they say things?

Student 1: Well, cause we, I think we go at a faster pace.

Student 2: Cause I've like, I've walked into a regular class and, like, they have, like, the teacher has to tell the students to like constantly be quiet and like, like just explaining, like, they'll be in like the same lesson.

Student 1: They don't really have an interest to learn, really.

Student 2: They're just there because they have to be.

Student 2's statement "Cause I've like, I've walked into a regular class and, like, they have, like, the teacher has to tell the students to like constantly be quiet" seems to articulate a transgression from one world to another. The student's statement "I've walked into a regular class" acts as if a "regular class" was alien territory inhabited by alien creatures ("regular students") who were primarily interested in talking ("the teacher has to tell the students to like constantly be quiet"). Student 1 then added to this image by claiming that these alien creatures "don't really have an interest to learn" and that, as Student 2 clarified, "they're just there because they have to be."

The different performance and effort expectations combined with the physical separation of students in GT classes to create what Margaret called a world within a world and what students called GT-land and GT-topia. In the focus group excerpt below, students explicitly articulated a difference in worlding:

Author: So is GT a group inside school? Or not?

Student 1: No, it's just like a class, like classes. Classes, but—

Student 2: I guess you could say that it's like a world difference, like it's GT-land

Student 3: It's so annoying

Author: GT-land. I like that. Tell me more.

Student 3: GT-topia.

Author: GT-land?

Student 2: Because it's like the GT, it's not like us GT people we don't, like, hang except for my other classes.

Student 1: It's like the people you're around with more, since sixth grade you're with the same people basically, so—

Student 3: Yeah, and kinda, like, lives in a bubble.

Students policed the boundaries of GT-land in sometimes dramatic ways. Both Margaret and Bill, in separate interview sessions, related the following anecdote. Due to logistical challenges one day, the teachers planned to combine GT with non-GT classes for a single day of social studies instruction. The GT student reaction was to skip school en masse that day: GT students apparently had no desire to comingle with students from outside of their world.

WHAT'S THE TAKEAWAY?

Why do these examples demonstrate that power is not a thing? These students didn't change anybody's thinking about what the GT label means. They didn't change any policies within the school. They didn't change how their teachers ran their classes. In fact, the teachers only learned about the students' thinking about the GT labels from conversations with this author. But the students still exerted power in that they exerted agency over their own understandings of their GT labels.

What makes this power so crucial for educators—and especially for educational researchers—is that it calls into question the trustworthiness of educational research that does not expansively capture students' fine-grained thinking. As one researcher puts it, "Groundbreaking results from one study could end up having very little generalizability to other groups of gifted individuals, depending on the definition used to identify the gifted in the original research."[24]

This study presents a new perspective on that claim: if researchers operationally define GT one way or just use a vague definition employed by a school district or other educational body or do not define GT at all but assume a shared meaning with readers, and students tacitly (because nobody asked them) define GT differently, would that difference in definitions impact the trustworthiness of the results of the study? The answer must be yes.

"Official" definitions of giftedness seem to continually change. Perhaps that's why researchers Hoge and Renzulli argue that "it is important, first, that researchers be explicit about their definition of giftedness. There is room for alternative definitions of giftedness, but it is important that the construct being used in the study be made explicit."[25] But it's not enough just for researchers to specify their understandings. Researchers must also dig deeply and listen carefully to students' thinking about the meaning of their labels.

If this study had imposed a definition for giftedness onto the school and the students being studied, potential discrepancies in meaning might never have been revealed between the definition of giftedness used by the study and the definitions circulating among the students. Everyone might have assumed, as most of the giftedness literature implies, that students hold stable understandings of giftedness. Yet within students' discourse in this study, little was fixed and stable about the content of the label.

The research methods used here seemed to make this power visible. By limiting students to single responses, questionnaires only capture students' thoughts within a particular and usually isolated moment. For example, a study by Kerr, Colangelo, and Gaeth asked GT students to complete an open-ended questionnaire.[26] One question asked students to complete the statement "Being gifted means." The authors of that study had apparently used this question to help determine the percentages of students who viewed giftedness in particular ways. The problem is that the question only captured students' feelings at that particular moment.

In contrast, this study analyzed the way students' discourse created narratives about the GT label over the span of many interviews and in a social setting, which allowed the students to bounce ideas off of each other and often even to complete each other's sentences. The social nature of the focus groups might have influenced students' responses, as well as the back and forth between researchers and students.

During these interviews, which really were just conversations, students often contradicted themselves as well as argued with each other about the points they were trying to make. Students made some of these contradictory statements in response to follow-up questions or comments, such as when this author challenged the students by saying, "But you're *GT*." Students also challenged each other's responses, such as when one student claimed, "Well, it's not like we have a choice," to which another student replied, "Well, we do have a choice."

Questionnaires and surveys do not, of course, contain these types of interactions. A survey question, however open-ended, only captures the thoughts or feelings that are in a student's head at a given moment. Researchers seem to assume that surveys will capture the same thoughts regardless of when the surveys are completed or of the conditions during which the surveys are completed. If that were the case, it wouldn't matter when or where the survey was completed, since students would give the same answer regardless of context.

For example, in a study by the researchers Graham, MacFadyen, and Richards, the authors explicitly state a preference for using survey over interview methods to measure students' perceptions of giftedness. That study focused on approximately the same age group of students as the students in the current study. It was given to seventy-eight students across two school settings, and it reports that students held positive feelings about giftedness labels. The authors claim "that learners of [that] age group would be more likely to respond positively and openly to an anonymous and short questionnaire."[27]

Perhaps. But as this study has shown, however, different thoughts or feelings about the GT label seem to be able to exist inside students' heads at different moments. This creates an important implication for researchers using survey methods: Which perceptions of the GT label do survey methods measure? Or, more precisely, which feelings or opinions are captured at which moment? And how are researchers to know which opinions or feelings are most accurate? Further, since trustworthiness of findings is so crucial to research, how are researchers to gauge the trustworthiness of possibly incomplete findings?

This study suggests that students might have given different answers to a question depending on circumstances and on the type of prompt used. Judging veracity and trustworthiness is always difficult. It's possible that, following the reasoning from Graham, MacFadyen, and Richards, the collaborative interviews with students made their responses less truthful than if they had answered in private. But the evidence doesn't suggest that. The checks and balances provided by other students, plus the repeated chances to respond, seem to generate more truthful responses, not less.

This question holds immense practical importance for education research and policy decisions based on large-scale data collection, which means practically all decisions made in or for schools. This study implies that students' perceptions of labels can be fluid, but survey methods usually give the opposite impression. This study does not claim that the Kerr, Colangelo, and Gaeth study or that quantitative data collection methods in general lack meaningfulness. Rather, it claims that such studies might not convey a complete picture.

What this means is that policy decisions for schools might be based on flawed assumptions—and educators might never know. In terms of power, the adults (the teachers, administrators, policymakers, and researchers) might not recognize students' power to hold complicated and nuanced understandings about their labels—because the adults never thought to create the conditions necessary to find out.

What might this look like in practice? Say a school district wants to know if their GT students hold a "growth" or a "fixed" mindset about "being GT."[28] Now say that the school district, out of efficiency, convenience, or just common practice, administers a survey to GT students to gauge their thoughts or that a district employee reads survey research regarding GT students' typical beliefs about mindsets. And say the school district implements a program based on that research.

According to this analysis of students' power, that school district program easily runs the risk of being wrong. The school district could mistakenly base its program on wrong assumptions about students' beliefs because the research supporting the program failed to capture students' in-depth thinking. Perhaps this results in the program not working as optimally as it otherwise could have. Perhaps the program actually causes problems for students, instead of helping them.

Now multiply this possibility across the country to thousands of school districts. Of course, no one can state whether this problem happens at a large scale—or if it happens at all. But the problem illustrates the tacit way that power works in this situation, as well as suggests the scope of problems potentially being caused by neglecting that power. This discussion of GT students' perceptions of their GT labels illustrates the sneaky ways that power can operate at what some might consider the lowest level in schools and how it can also create big problems for schools.

NOTES

1. In 2022 high school students walked out of school for a variety of reasons, including protesting mask mandates (in CA, IL, and WA), gun violence (in CA, MI, NY, and VA), and school conditions during Covid-19 (in NY).

2. The data used in this chapter were initially published in the following article: Bryan Meadows and Jacob W. Neumann, "What does it mean to assess gifted students' perceptions of giftedness labels?" *Interchange* 48, no. 2 (May 2017): 145–65.

3. The school district in which this study was conducted used four criteria to evaluate giftedness in students in grades 6 through 11: teacher observations, student products, mental ability test scores, and achievement test scores. Teacher observations were intended to measure students' characteristics regarding learning and motivation. The student products consisted of a written essay and a mathematics assessment. Both products were scored by a team of GT teachers from across the school district. For the mental ability tests, students were administered the Otis Lennon School Ability Test and the Naglieri Non-Verbal Ability Test. Students were given a reading and a mathematics portion of the Iowa Test of Basic Skills for the achievement measure.

4. Giftedness was initially defined with a focus on intellectual ability as measured by IQ tests, according to Terman. More recently, giftedness has been defined by Dai (in 2009) as a "result of the confluence of several forces . . . coming together in the right place at the right time." Indeed, as Dai puts it (in 2010), "the field of gifted education has long been plagued by the issue of how to define giftedness and gifted students." See Lewis Terman, *Genetic studies of genius: Mental and physical traits of a thousand gifted children* (Stanford, CA: Stanford University Press, 1926); David Y. Dai, "Essential tensions surrounding the concept of giftedness," in *International handbook of giftedness*, ed. Larissa Shavinina (Houten, The Netherlands: Springer, 2009), 46; and David Y. Dai, *The nature and nurture of giftedness: A new framework for understanding gifted education* (New York: Teachers College Press, 2010), 227.

5. Jiri Mudrak and Katerina Zabrodska, "Childhood giftedness, adolescent agency: A systemic multiple-case study," *Gifted Child Quarterly* 59, no. 1 (November 2014): 57.

6. Gary A. Davis and Sylvia B. Rimm, *Education of the gifted and talented*, 5th ed. (Boston: Allyn & Bacon, 2004).

7. Herbert W. Marsh et al., "The effects of gifted and talented programs on academic self-concept: The big fish strikes again," *American Educational Research Journal* 32, no. 2 (Summer 1995): 285–319; and Tracey L. Cross, Laurence J. Coleman, and Marge Terhaar-Yonkers, "The social cognition of gifted adolescents in schools: Managing the stigma of giftedness," *Journal for the Education of the Gifted* 15, no. 1 (October 1991): 44–55.

8. John F. Feldhusen and David Y. Dai, "Gifted students' attitudes and perceptions of the gifted label, special programs, and peer relations," *Journal of Secondary Gifted Education* 9, no. 1 (August 1997): 15–20.

9. Barbara Kerr, Nicholas Colangelo, and Julie Gaeth, "Gifted adolescents' attitudes toward their giftedness," *Gifted Child Quarterly* 32, no. 2 (April 1988): 246.

10. Matthew C. Makel et al., "Gifted students' implicit beliefs about intelligence and giftedness," *Gifted Child Quarterly* 59, no. 4 (August 2015): 202–13.

11. Samuel L. Guskin et al., "Being labeled gifted or talented: Meanings and effects perceived by students in special programs," *Gifted Child Quarterly* 3, no. 2 (Spring 1986): 64.

12. Mark A. Kunkel et al., "The experience of giftedness: A concept map," *Gifted Child Quarterly* 39, no. 3 (July 1995): 130.

13. Kunkel et al., "The experience of giftedness," 130.

14. Thomas M. Buescher, "A framework for understanding the social and emotional development of gifted and talented adolescents," *Roeper Review* 8, no. 1 (1985): 10–15; Laurence J. Coleman and Tracey L. Cross, "Is being gifted a social handicap?" *Journal for the Education of the Gifted* 11, no. 4 (July 1988): 41–56; Laurence J. Coleman and Michael D. Sanders, "Understanding the needs of gifted students: Social needs, social choices and masking one's giftedness," *Journal of Secondary Gifted Education* 5, no. 1 (January 1993): 22–25; Cross, Coleman, and Terhaar-Yonkers, "The social cognition of gifted adolescents in schools," 44–55; and Amy Robinson, "Does that describe me? Adolescents' acceptance of the gifted label," *Journal for the Education of the Gifted* 13 (1990): 245–55.

15. Coleman and Sanders, "Understanding the needs of gifted students," 23–24.

16. Coleman and Cross, "Is being gifted a social handicap?" 41.

17. This study investigated GT students' perceptions of the GT label in two eighth-grade US history classrooms. These classes were located in a mid-sized city in South Texas. At the time of this study, the school enrolled approximately 1200 students in grades 6 through 8, and its enrollment was 88 percent Latino, 8 percent White, 3 percent Asian, and 1 percent Black. This study was conducted in two teachers' classrooms. At the time of the study, one teacher, Ms. Rhodes, had taught US history for twenty years, and the other, Mr. Trammell, had taught it for eight years. Twenty-five students (13 in one class and 12 in the other) agreed to participate in individual and focus group interviews for this study. These students self-selected to participate in that they were the only students out of 58 students between the two classes to return signed parental consent forms. Sixteen of these students were female and 9 were male. Further, of the 25 students, 24 identified themselves as Latino/a, and one identified himself as White.

In terms of the mechanics of the study, this researcher visited each classroom one to two times per week for one class period each, for a total of approximately ninety hours of observation over the course of one school year. In order to get as close to the phenomenon as possible, data collection focused on students' and teachers' discourse in regular classroom activities, formal interviews with students and with the teachers, and informal conversations with the teachers. Over the course of the study, observations included a range of daily classroom activities, including large group discussions, small group activities, independent practice, review activities, quizzes and tests, and teacher lectures. Nonparticipant-observer field notes and audio recordings were made of regular classroom activities. Additionally, informal, three-to-five minute conversations were had with each teacher either before or after each observation.

Eight semi-structured interviews were conducted with all students, both individually and in small focus groups of between three and five students, and five semi-structured interviews were conducted with the two teachers, three with one and two with the other. The interviews with students lasted approximately thirty minutes each, and the teacher interviews lasted approximately forty-five minutes each. All interviews were conducted between March and June of 2016.

18. Tracey L. Cross, Laurence J. Coleman, and Roger A. Stewart, "The social cognition of gifted adolescents: An exploration of the stigma of giftedness paradigm," *Roeper Review* 16, no. 1 (1993): 37–40; Feldhusen and Dai, "Gifted students' attitudes," 15–20; Kerr, Colangelo, and Gaeth, "Gifted adolescents," 245–47; Kunkel et al., "The experience of giftedness," 126–34; Makel et al., "Gifted students implicit beliefs," 202–13; and Rochelle Manor-Bullock, Christine Look, and David N. Dixon, "Is giftedness socially stigmatizing? The impact of high achievement on social interactions," *Journal for the Education of the Gifted* 18, no. 3 (July 1995): 319–38.

19. The interviews were semi-structured in that they were organized around particular topics, but they didn't have a predetermined set of questions for each participant. Instead, referencing Agar's work, each interview flowed organically through a number of "question-asking strategies" focused on several topics: how students defined GT; their perspectives on classroom activities, homework, and teacher expectations; how GT classes differed from non-GT classes; what the social aspect of having a GT label was like; and how they felt about their GT classes and status. In the interviews with teachers, questions focused on clarifying, explaining, or expanding on observations made in their classrooms or on comments students had made during interviews.

Four main question-asking strategies facilitated the interviews with students. First, students were asked to define structures, programs, and activities, but this was done in ways that suggested that this researcher did not know the answer. Second, follow-up questions asked students to extend their responses. Third, students' responses were challenged. Fourth, students were asked about their feelings. These strategies helped to gain, as Agar writes, a deeper "insider's perspective" into the students' perceptions of the GT label.

All interviews were transcribed and, along with field notes, analyzed using coding/memoing methods (from Corbin and Strauss) to identify emergent concepts and themes. Coding happened on several levels. First coded were all instances in field notes and interview transcripts of students and/or teachers articulating or implying a definition of GT. Second, marked notes and transcripts were analyzed for themes. Third, relevant field note and transcript data were grouped into the identified themes. See Michael H. Agar, *The professional stranger: An informal introduction to ethnography*, 2nd ed. (Bingley, UK: Emerald Group Publishing, 2008); and Juliet Corbin and Anselm Strauss, *Basics of qualitative research*, 3rd ed. (Los Angeles: Sage, 2008).

20. Coleman and Sanders, "Understanding the needs of gifted students," 22–25; Coleman and Cross, "Is being gifted a social handicap?" 41–56; Cross, Coleman,

Terhaar-Yonkers, "The social cognition of gifted adolescents in schools," 44–55; and Cross, Coleman, and Stewart, "The social cognition of gifted adolescents," 37–40.

21. For example, Kerr, Colangelo, and Gaeth find that, of the students they studied, 64 percent viewed giftedness in terms of performance, and 36 percent viewed it as a trait. See Kerr, Colangelo, and Gaeth, "Gifted adolescents," 245–247.

22. Hugh Mehan, "The construction of an LD student: A case study in the politics of representation," in *Discourse theory and practice: A reader*, ed. Margaret Wetherell, Stephanie Taylor, and Simeon Yates (London: Sage, 2001), 356.

23. This narrative resembled Dweck's "entity" theory of learning, and it seemed similar to general conceptions of giftedness, except that students articulated this difference in vague terms of perception, not innate intelligence. See Carol S. Dweck, "Mindsets and human nature: Promoting change in the Middle East, the schoolyard, the racial divide, and willpower," *American Psychologist* 67, no. 8 (November 2012): 614–22.

24. Carol Carman, "Comparing apples and oranges: Fifteen years of definitions of giftedness in research," *Journal of Advanced Academics* 24, no. 1 (February 2013): 53.

25. Robert D. Hoge and Joseph S. Renzulli, "Exploring the link between giftedness and self-concept," *Review of Educational Research* 63, no. 4 (Winter 1993): 460.

26. Kerr, Colangelo, and Gaeth, "Gifted adolescents."

27. Suzanne Graham, Tony MacFadyen, and Brian Richards, "Learners' perceptions of being identified as very able: Insights from modern foreign languages and physical education," *Journal of Curriculum Studies* 44, no. 3 (May 2012): 331.

28. Carol. S. Dweck, *Mindset: The new psychology for success* (New York: Ballantine Books, 2006).

Chapter 4

The Tension between High-Stakes Testing and Teachers' Knowledge

Chapter 4 analyzes the second part of the definition of power: power is not linear. How teachers teach, what content they choose to teach, how quickly or slowly they teach that content, what types of learning activities or processes they use, how student-centered or teacher-centered their teaching is, and what types of assessments they use are all influenced by many factors. Two of the biggest factors are high-stakes testing and teachers' personal knowledge and beliefs about teaching.

These two factors can be thought of as iterations of power. High-stakes testing changes how teachers teach. It imposes constraints on teachers' instruction. Public school teachers cannot ignore it; indeed, in most schools, high-stakes testing scores are the primary currency in teacher evaluations. However, teachers also exert their own power over their teaching. This power is based on their personal knowledge and beliefs about teaching. Like high-stakes testing, their knowledge and beliefs also impact how they organize content, how they frame questions to students, how they assess students, and more. Each decision is an act of power.

Neither of these factors operates linearly on teachers' work. Instead, they operate almost haphazardly as teachers respond to and make day-to-day decisions about their teaching. Power here doesn't flow; it pops up, driven by circumstance, by context, by need, and by preference. The factors also pull at each other. Sometimes high-stakes testing dominates; other times, their knowledge and beliefs do. But the factors always mediate each other as teachers struggle to meet often competing demands, what Cheryl Craig calls "feeding two dragons"—the demands of high-stakes testing and teachers' own goals for their students' learning.[1]

This chapter takes a fine-grained look at this tension through the experiences of Margaret, Bill, and Mary, three of the social studies teachers at Connors Middle School. You will see how high-stakes testing imposed power over their teaching and, at the same time, that the teachers exerted their own power over their teaching. But you won't see any flows of power. The back-and-forth tension doesn't signal opposite power flows. Rather, it demonstrates the contingent and often reactionary nature of power in schools. Power here isn't linear; it's used toward particular ends.

ESTABLISHING CONTEXT: A BRIEF REVIEW OF THE RESEARCH LITERATURE

Although education researchers have been studying it for decades, no consensus exists as to a dominant influence between high-stakes testing and teachers' knowledge and beliefs. Instead, this short review explains the range of perspectives that researchers hold about these different influences. These literature bases also demonstrate conflicting examples of power, further supporting the contention that power in schools is not linear.

Brief Review: The Influence of High-Stakes Accountability Testing on Teachers' Work

Much of the literature on high-stakes accountability testing holds that high-stakes testing not only has a deleterious effect on teaching but also is the primary influence on teaching.[2] This line of research argues that high-stakes testing narrows teachers' pedagogical options, compelling teacher-centered practices in the classroom. Indeed, one researcher contends that high-stakes testing acts as a form of labor control over teachers' work.[3] Another writes, "Because multiple-choice testing leads to multiple-choice teaching, the methods that teachers have in their arsenal become reduced, and teaching work is deskilled."[4]

Several studies of high-stakes testing describe how high-stakes testing often narrows teachers' pedagogical options, creating what several researchers have called testing dilemmas for teachers.[5] The researchers Valli and Buese describe it, saying, "Because the curriculum moved at such a fast pace and because the topics were organized in such an unfamiliar way, teachers felt as though they were racing through it. Several teachers referred to the deterioration of their pedagogies into what they called 'hit or miss' and 'drive-by' teaching."[6] This pacing problem is compounded by the fact that social studies teachers often have to "deal with a high-stakes curriculum that is notoriously 'a mile wide and an inch deep.'"[7] It's further suggested that the pacing rush causes teachers to employ teacher-centered methods in their classrooms.[8]

Still other researchers have called this effect a "just the facts, ma'am" influence on teaching.[9] A number of studies provide evidence that support this pedagogical narrowing effect of high-stakes testing.[10] For example, the researchers Faulkner and Cook have found that middle school teachers in Kentucky "felt strongly that the [high-stakes] assessment weighed heavily on their minds" and "resorted to 'coverage' over in-depth study of instructional topics."[11]

However, a number of researchers offer a different view of the effects of high-stakes testing and present evidence of teachers teaching in meaningful and productive ways despite high-stakes accountability testing. For example, some researchers illustrate how teachers find ways to develop constructivist classrooms even within high-stakes testing environments.[12] Other studies show how teachers are able to generate "thoughtfulness" in the classroom,[13] even if time for such thinking is squeezed by high-stakes testing.[14]

Brief Review: The Influence of Teachers' Knowledge and Beliefs on Their Work

The influence of teachers' knowledge and beliefs has been studied in a variety of ways separate from comparisons with high-stakes testing. It is well established that teachers' knowledge and beliefs influence their work.[15] The literature on teachers' beliefs is broad, so broad, indeed, that one scholar suggests that "one way to get a handle on the literature of teacher belief is to recognize it as a cluster of separate research agendas."[16] This literature ranges from the influence on self-efficacy to convictions about teaching methods,[17] from subject matter to teaching struggling readers.[18]

Jean Clandinin and Michael Connelly, well-known narrative researchers, describe teachers' knowledge as "personal practical knowledge" that operates within a "professional knowledge landscape."[19] Personal practical knowledge "is knowledge that reflects the individual's prior knowledge and acknowledges the contextual nature of a teacher's knowledge."[20] Teachers' personal practical knowledge is lived in professional knowledge landscapes that shape what counts as "effective teaching, what teachers know, what knowledge is seen as essential for teaching and who is warranted to produce knowledge about teaching."[21]

Teachers' knowledge and beliefs influence the way they teach. Kagan claims that "researchers have found that a teacher's beliefs usually reflect the actual nature of the instruction the teacher provides to students."[22] For example, in a previous research study, one middle school social studies teacher extensively used drama in her teaching, what she called "act it outs," because she felt that such participatory and experiential activities helped her students gain more in-depth understanding of historical events.[23]

Teachers' beliefs about teaching are difficult to change. For example, Deborah Britzman argues that teacher education programs typically reinforce teacher candidates' already existing beliefs about teaching rather than help candidates to develop new ones.[24] Once they begin work as teachers of record, "teachers continue to solve instructional problems largely by relying on their own beliefs and experiences" rather than "by reading and applying the findings of educational research."[25]

Two other areas of teachers' beliefs also influence their work: what Fred Newmann calls the American "addiction to coverage" and the widespread belief in what Mary Metz calls "Real School."[26] These beliefs are linked to classroom teaching through societal values regarding the structure of knowledge and the institution of schools. These dominant schooling patterns hold broad institutional significance and resist easy alteration in the public mind.[27]

According to Newmann, the addiction to content coverage is a fundamental reason that teachers employ teacher-centered practices that rush through the formal curriculum. Newmann claims that a variety of negative consequences result from this focus on coverage: content that is quickly learned and even more quickly forgotten; a reinforced habit of mindlessness; conditioning students to *not* ask thoughtful questions; and, of course, a brief survey rather than in-depth focus on meaning.[28]

The belief in "real school" also helps to explain some of the consistency found in public schools across the country. By "real school," Metz means patterns and practices of schooling that are publicly, even if tacitly, considered to be real, authentic, and appropriate. Put differently, "real schools" and, thus, "real teachers," are publicly expected to engage in particular types of behaviors and practices because that is what "real schools and teachers" do. These patterns of schooling are often publicly considered to be "just the way schools are."[29]

Indeed, Metz argues that secondary schools seem to follow a common script. She claims that the rituals of "real school" are symbols of equity that exert a powerful tug on the American psyche. In the national consciousness, notions of equal opportunity tightly connect to the impulse to provide all students with the *same* education—even if "the public [also] perceives schools to be in practice very *un*equal."[30] Thus, "the common script and its enactment with symbols and rituals of Real School . . . gives a skeletal reality to the claim of equity through sameness":[31] "Its enactment assures both participants and outsiders of the equity of public schooling as a whole, while it certifies teachers and students who follow it as legitimate and worthy participants in the academic and social life of the broader society. Participation in the drama it sketches out is participation in a ritual that affirms membership in mainstream American life."[32]

In other words, teachers continue to follow and, thus, tacitly endorse, the common script not just in reaction to institutional pressures but also from an emotional desire to fit into mainstream notions about what it means to be a teacher. Thus, while teachers can feel public pressure to comply with expected behaviors of teachers, this belief in "real school" is also very much a value claim on the part of teachers. They follow the range of endorsed behaviors in part because those behaviors represent what it means to be a "real teacher" who teaches in a "real school."

THE ACCOUNTABILITY CONTEXT IN TEXAS

Since this chapter focuses in part on high-stakes accountability testing, it is helpful to briefly describe the accountability context in Texas. Beginning in 1980, Texas has progressed through five versions of statewide accountability exams: the TABS (Texas Assessment of Basic Skills) from 1980 to 1985; the TEAMS (Texas Educational Assessment of Minimum Skills) from 1986 to 1989; the TAAS (Texas Assessment of Academic Skills) from 1990 to 2002; the TAKS (Texas Assessment of Knowledge and Skills) from 2003 to 2011; and the STAAR (State of Texas Assessments of Academic Readiness), which was implemented in the 2011–2012 school year.

According to the Texas Education Agency (TEA), each subsequent exam builds upon its predecessor in terms of scope, complexity, and rigor. According to TEA, the STAAR represents a marked increase in scope, complexity, and rigor from the previous test, the TAKS.[33] Below are a few claims made by TEA about the new test:

- "STAAR will represent a more unified, comprehensive assessment program that will incorporate more rigorous college and career readiness standards."
- "Performance standards will be set so that they require a higher level of student performance than is required on the current TAKS assessments."
- "Assessments will increase in length at most grade levels and subjects, and overall test difficulty will be increased by including more rigorous [test] items."
- "The rigor of the [test] items will be increased by assessing skills at a greater depth and level of cognitive complexity."[34]

Eighth-grade students in Texas take high-stakes accountability exams in reading, mathematics, science, and social studies. During the timeframe of this study, students needed to pass the reading and mathematics exams to advance to the next grade. The social studies and science exams, however, were not required for eighth graders to advance to ninth grade. Some researchers have noted, however, that teachers can feel pressure from standardized testing, not from just consequences and rewards but simply because that testing is high-stakes.[35]

STORIES OF POWER THAT PULL ON TEACHERS' WORK

The following sections tell stories about how the teachers at Connors wrestled with the tensions between high-stakes testing and their personal knowledge and beliefs about teaching. The first section focuses on four stories about specific elements of the tension with high-stakes testing: average yearly progress (AYP), the pacing problem, the testing apparatus, and the structure of the exam itself. The second section examines particular examples of how the teachers' knowledge and beliefs shaped their decision making about content, lesson design, and students' learning.

Influence of High-stakes Accountability Testing

Think of these stories as stories about power. The teachers exerted power over their teaching in specific ways. But AYP, the pacing problem, the testing apparatus, and the structure of the exam also exerted power on their teaching. These factors can be described as "influences," but they can only influence *because* they exert power. And these examples of power do not flow. Instead, they emanate from policies, practices, and preferences that shape the teachers' work in complex ways.

AYP

AYP exerts power on teachers' work at Connors in a variety of ways. At one point during the study, Bill Trammell claimed, "This year is mostly different because of AYP. That has had the biggest effect on our campus, and because the district is going through its issues with AYP, it all rolls downhill to schools. We did not make AYP last year. So things have changed on a global scale, because our district is having these issues and they're having to implement new things and new ideas."

One productive way to conceptualize the changes wrought by the school's failure to meet AYP is through the notions of "stories of school" and "teacher stories."[36] Stories of school are stories told about a school by people such as school board members, school administrators, parents and community members, and even by teachers. These stories portray the school as imbued with qualities that invested parties try hard to maintain. Teacher stories, on the other hand, are stories that teachers live and tell about their teaching work.

At times these different stories coexist seamlessly and even support each other. But when a story of school is changed or threatened, the tension within and around the challenged story of school can profoundly influence the teacher stories that its teachers live and tell about their work. The story of Connors had been one of enviable success since its opening in 2000. Serving an affluent area of the city and school district, the school earned numerous academic, athletic, musical, and other extracurricular awards. It had even been recognized by various business organizations and statewide publishing organizations for its academic achievement.

But early in the 2010s, two things happened that threatened Connors' story of itself: (1) the state of Texas changed its high-stakes accountability exam from the TAKS to the STAAR (see above), and (2) the AYP requirements were raised to 87 percent passing on the English/language arts (ELA) exam and to 83 percent passing on the mathematics exam. Soon after, Connors failed to meet the new standards in both ELA and mathematics. This failure, along with the well-known but now-threatened story of school that Connors enjoyed in the local community, caused a wave of ripples that influenced multiple aspects of its teachers' work.

The Pacing Problem

Perhaps the most visceral influence of AYP for these social studies teachers was the perennial pacing problem. Numerous studies recount how the pacing of curriculum (and the concomitant problem of curriculum alignment) can strongly influence teachers' work.[37] The pacing problem at Connors was compounded by its status as an International Baccalaureate (IB) school. IB programs provide advanced curriculum and assessment standards for students, and they are often publicly held in high esteem.

The teachers at Connors, then, were effectively ruled by two masters. One master, the school district curriculum plan for each grade level, plotted a curriculum sprint for teachers and students. Bill Trammell recounted to me one of the effects of the TAKS (the high-stakes accountability exam in effect at the time): "I must do the mile wide and inch-deep type approach because I'm given all these criteria and all these objectives, and it's such a sprint from the first day of school all the way to the TAKS test." Since failing to meet AYP, teachers felt this pressure even more strongly.

The other master, the school's IB guidelines, stressed what the teachers referred to as depth and complexity. A tenet of the IB Middle Years Program is sustained inquiry which, according to the International Baccalaureate website, helps "students become creative, critical, and reflective thinkers."[38] This curriculum promotes prolonged, reflective engagement with issues and ideas.

The competing pulls by these two forces, one toward coverage, the other toward sustained inquiry, created constant tension for the teachers.

Thus, when teachers discussed pacing pressures, those pressures were always accompanied by IB pressures. For example, Mary Watson shared the following:

> On the one hand, we want to make our curriculum work for the kids, and then CSCOPE (what teachers called the school district curriculum guidelines) pacing wants us to rush through every two weeks to something different. And at the same time, we keep in mind our IB curriculum. So we've got to work with the state TEKS [the state high-stakes curriculum, called the Texas Essential Knowledge and Skills], work with CSCOPE that's supposed to be aligned to the TEKS, the pacing that doesn't necessarily agree with how we think works for the kids. The scope and sequence is crazy; two weeks on every subject and then move on.

The pacing problem directly and continuously exerted power on these teachers' work. Margaret Rhodes explained that the pacing problem sometimes caused her to "teach like an auctioneer. And so a lot of it is teacher directed." After the AYP problem, Margaret lamented that even more of her teaching was limited to more teacher-directed methods:

> *Margaret:* The problem is CSCOPE follows the YAG, year at a glance. To me, they want depth and complexity, but if you follow the year at a glance, and you try to get to Jackson by Christmas, how can you do any depth? How can you do "the government, one week" [snaps her fingers]?
>
> *Jacob:* You get to Jackson, when, February?
>
> *Margaret:* I get there January-ish. I sped up this year. I didn't do Washington crossing the Delaware; I didn't do the debate with Madison.
>
> *Jacob:* You didn't have them make the boat?
>
> *Margaret:* No, I didn't do any of it. I had to chop it up, because these district assessments, if you show up short, "What's going on on your campus?"

Margaret was well-known and respected for creatively utilizing drama in her classroom to help students wrestle with a range of complex historical events and ideas. When she taught the English Civil War, for example, she even dressed up in costume as a queen and used characters and props (complete with a balloon-shaped axe) to engage students in this period of history. Yet because of the pacing problem, she was forced to eliminate many of the dramatic structures she knew to be effective and engaging for students.

The Testing Apparatus

Compounding the pacing problem was the influence of the "testing apparatus." The testing apparatus combined with the pacing problem to further restrict teachers' instructional time with students, time that was needed to generate the depth and complexity called for by IB and by these teachers' beliefs about teaching. The testing apparatus is the battery of exams, both practice and real, affiliated with high-stakes testing, that the state and school district give to students each year.

In Connors' school district, this battery of exams could consume several weeks of instructional time each year. Combined with the fact that high-stakes testing in social studies in Texas happens in April, the testing apparatus left social studies teachers approximately two-thirds of the school year to prepare students for the exam. Margaret spoke extensively about the influence of the testing apparatus. About the testing apparatus, she claimed: "[It] doesn't impact what I teach, but it does impact how I teach it. I have a wealth of training and materials, and I'll sometimes think, can't do that this year, not enough time. You have to pick the activities you think will give the most value."

Margaret's argument was not against accountability. She claimed that she "firmly believes" in holding teachers accountable for their students' learning. But she voiced consistent exasperation at the testing apparatus that robbed her of valuable instructional time. In the excerpt below, Margaret discussed these frustrations at length:

> *Jacob:* You once said, "I'm a fan of accountability, but I think we can do it in better ways."
>
> *Margaret:* Exactly. I firmly believe in accountability. You have to have accountability. What you can't have is . . . my biggest concern with TAKS is that you lose so much instructional time preparing for the tests. It's a function of the test. The way we are doing it eats up too much instructional time. It's kind of like you're robbing Peter to pay Paul. What could I do with those two or three weeks with these kids? So here's the funny part. They call you in. They say you need to do *this*. We know that. Our question is when. How would we fit that in? It's not that we don't get that. It's just, when you're blocking off days for testing, that's instructional time that could be used for that very thing. And it used to be worse! The district . . . the benchmarks, my god, you know? You'd get started on something . . . The district has cut back on that because teachers were just saying, if we're working on testing for three weeks, that's half a six weeks! Percentage-wise, that's a big chunk of the year.

Teachers always make selective choices about how to allocate their instructional time with students. By further limiting their instructional time with students, the testing apparatus exaggerated this demand on teachers. When asked about things they would like to do with students if they had more time, Margaret claimed, "I would like to do more debates. I would like to give them more time to talk. Time to kinda let it settle in. But because we move so fast, there's no time to do that in class." Bill Trammell offered a different focus, but one that also required time to "dig in" to subject matter: "Well, building a government would be something I would love to get into more detail about. To have students try to build their own government and to go through all the pitfalls to see what they would come up with, to see how similar or dissimilar it turns out to be with what happened with the colonists and, later, with the Constitutional Convention."

The combination of the pacing problem and the testing apparatus caused serious professional and emotional discomfort among the teachers. Margaret and Mary Watson expressed similar frustrations. Here is Mary Watson: "It's exhausting. The state tests students to death, and the district doubles and triples what the state's going to do to be ready for the state test! I think that we could use our time better; if we're constantly measuring them, when do we help students grow between the measures?"

Margaret explained her frustration in a similar fashion: "So there was this pressure every six weeks to be *here*, and I was never quite up there. So that creates friction problems. And then it comes down to how many days of teaching [for testing] are we giving up now? And I can't . . . it's like I feel like I'm . . . these kids trust me to teach it well, and I feel like I'm forced . . . and I could be wrong. See, that's the thing; I'm not the boss. I really feel like they think this is the answer. But from my perspective, from the way I teach, it doesn't work for me."

When Margaret referred to district assessments, benchmarks, and the pressure every six weeks to be "*here*," she was referring to the district-made assessments administered to students each grading period (in this case, every six weeks). Margaret shared the following:

> The emphasis is no longer about learning; it's about the testing and passing. And because of AYP, it's been kicked into high gear. Now there's this move towards lockstep teaching, everybody on the same page, the creativity's kind of . . . they want us to be creative, but the reality of it is, you really can't. I personally don't have the stamina to teach the way it needs to be taught. I feel so strongly about my teaching methods that I don't think I can see myself teaching another way.

This is an example of the school district using assessment to monitor teachers' compliance with the district policy regarding pacing. The lack of trust that Margaret mentioned arguably applied to the school district's relationship to its teachers. After being imposed with strict pacing demands that were often enforced by benchmark tests and six-weeks assessments, the teachers were also expected to be, according to Bill Trammell,

> aligned to the direction the superintendent wants to go in terms of everybody's on the same page, everybody's following roughly the same outline in their classes. That is very different than [in] previous years. Because there were differences in the schools when it came to how closely they followed the curriculum that is recommended. They were all doing TEKS [the state curriculum], but they were doing it their own way. Now with CSCOPE you have an outline you can build from, but you're expected to hit certain marks by certain times.

Thus, as research into high-stakes testing illustrates, the breadth of social studies curriculums can be challenging enough to teach and learn in one school year. The testing apparatus made that problem even more difficult by compressing teachers' time for teaching this broad swath of content into an even shorter timeframe. This, of course, created an ongoing tension between the power of testing and all that accompanies testing to change how teachers teach and the power of the teachers' own desires for their teaching.

The Structure of the Exam

The structure of the two high-stakes exams in effect during this study created different power influences on the teachers' work. In Texas, only eighth-grade students take a high-stakes exam for social studies (US history), so only eighth-grade teachers are directly influenced by the exam. Sixth- and seventh-grade teachers, however, feel indirect influences due to test-related spillover. In the name of consistency, school administrators in this school district assigned sixth- and seventh-grade teachers and students similar testing benchmarks.

According to the teachers, the TAKS heavily emphasized factual recall and recognition, what Margaret called the bare bones. For example, Margaret claimed that the structure of the TAKS influenced how she tried to reach her students: "The testing forces you to teach to the bottom. When you have bright kids, you know they are going to pass. They read the book; they answer the questions. So you're really just forced to go to those bubble kids, the kids who could go either way. And the lower ones, the ones at the bottom, you just hope they pass."

To help the "bubble kids" and those at the bottom, Margaret began her teaching with stripped-down content, what she called the bare bones. Margaret argued that because the exam tested students' ability to remember such a wide range of random and isolated facts, she must organize course content into simplified chunks that were easy for her students to digest and remember.

In the following interview excerpt, Margaret interpreted the effect of the structure of the exam on history content in her class. The interview excerpt specifically refers to handouts that she gave to students (an example of which is found in figure 4.1), which provides a vivid illustration of this common practice Margaret used to condense information for students:

Jacob: In looking at the handouts that you give to the students, especially the cartoons and the charts, if we cut out the boxes [that divide and organize

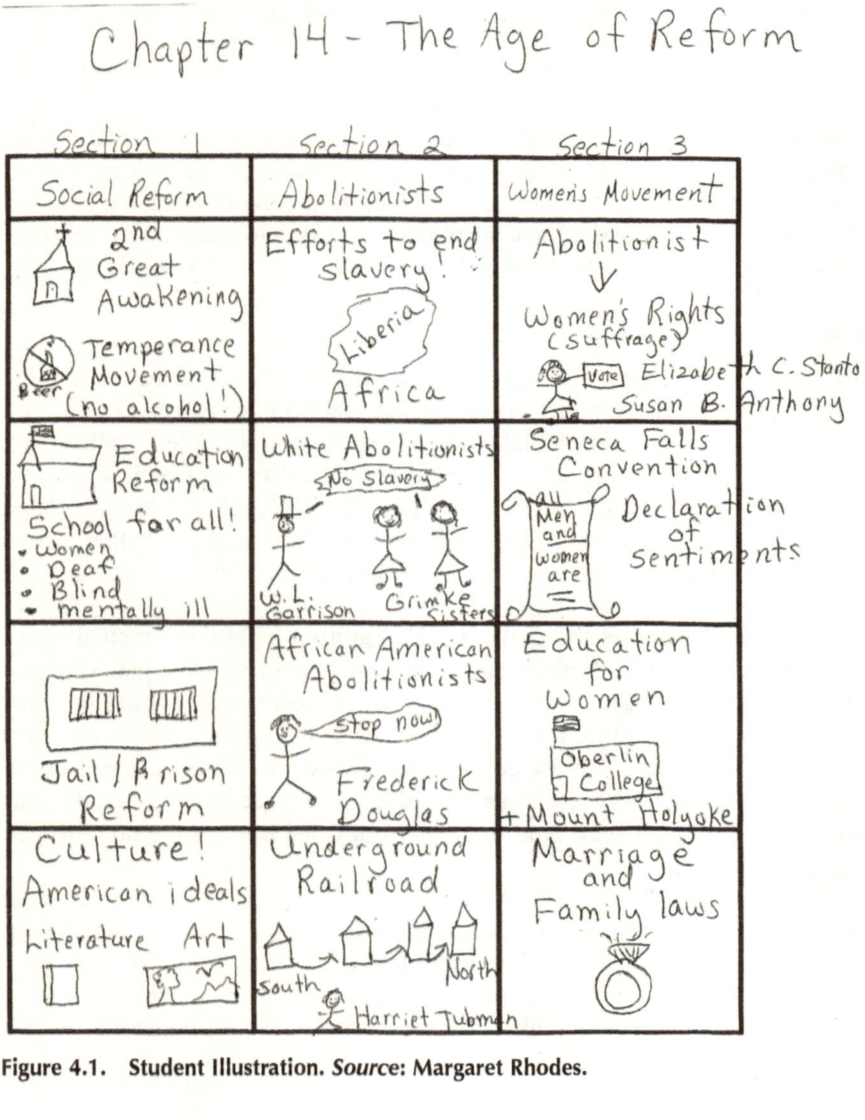

Chapter 14 – The Age of Reform

Section 1	Section 2	Section 3
Social Reform	Abolitionists	Women's Movement
2nd Great Awakening / Temperance Movement (no alcohol!)	Efforts to end slavery! / Liberia / Africa	Abolitionist ↓ Women's Rights (suffrage) / Elizabeth C. Stanton / Susan B. Anthony
Education Reform / School for all! • Women • Deaf • Blind • mentally ill	White Abolitionists / No Slavery / W. L. Garrison / Grimke Sisters	Seneca Falls Convention / All Men and Women are = / Declaration of Sentiments
Jail / Prison Reform	African American Abolitionists / Stop now! / Frederick Douglas	Education for Women / Oberlin College / Mount Holyoke
Culture! / American ideals / Literature Art	Underground Railroad / South / North / Harriet Tubman	Marriage and Family laws

Figure 4.1. Student Illustration. *Source:* Margaret Rhodes.

information on the handout], it kind of looks like currency. Kind of like historical currency.

Margaret: Yeah, it kind of does.

Jacob: And if we were to only look at this stuff, it looks like a gloss, just a sheen . . .

Margaret: Snap-shots.

Jacob: Boiled-down information.

Margaret: Bare-bones. TAKS is the bare bones.

Jacob: There's a connection there?

Margaret: Ummhmm.

Jacob: So it's fair to say there's a connection between TAKS and boiling down concepts for students to help them understand . . . *Marbury v. Madison*, two lines . . .

Margaret: Done.

Jacob: You'll go into depth in other ways; you make lots of connections. But in terms of presenting information in graphic organizers . . .

Margaret: You have to condense it to the important points. Then you can get out into debate, the activities. But they have to have that skeleton. That has to be there, just so that they can have a frame of reference, the dates, the order of events, that kind of thing. So I start with graphic organizers.

Another example of the TAKS compelling teachers to pare down content to the bare bones was found when Margaret taught the Civil War. Before TAKS, Margaret spent five days, one for each year of the war, covering basic information. For each day/year, Margaret lectured over material she thought to be essential, which was listed on handouts she gave the students. For example, for 1863, the handout shows cartoon-style drawings of the first US Red Cross, Clara Barton, the Battles of Gettysburg and Vicksburg, and the Gettysburg Address (see figure 4.2).

After TAKS, however, Margaret had her students examine the war in more depth. For example, students performed a play on Lincoln's assassination; she lingered in longer class discussions over connections between the Civil War and Reconstruction; and she assigned students a museum project over the Civil War in which students worked in groups to make a museum exhibit about an aspect of their choice about the war (students would select a range of topics from women spies to specific battles to Civil War–era fashion). She spent equal class time on the two halves, but each part took a drastically different approach to content and to learning.

Chapter 4

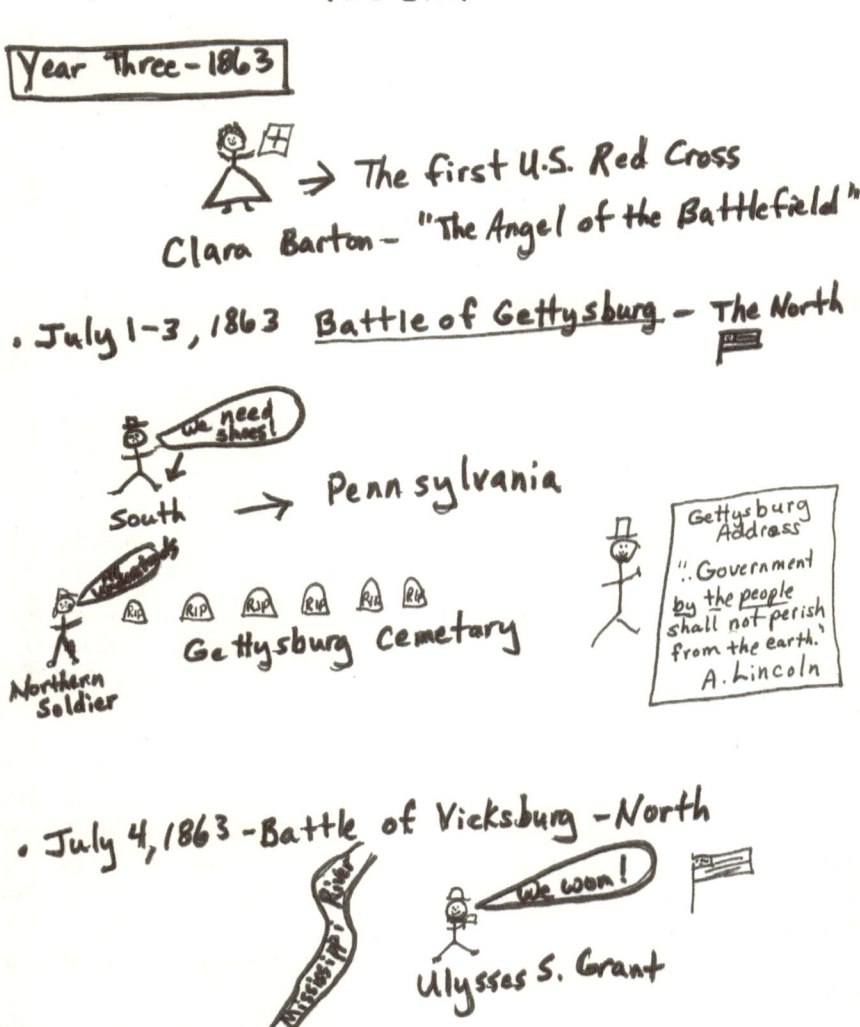

Figure 4.2. Student Illustration. *Source*: Margaret Rhodes.

The influence of the STAAR exam, on the other hand, was more difficult to gauge. The feeling among the teachers was that the test would compel teachers to rethink their teaching. As Bill Trammell put it, "the thing is, with the new test, it's going to have to change." Eighth-grade students took a district-made six-weeks test, a summative exam at the end of each grading period. Bill Trammell shared, "I can understand why they're trying to make it STAAR-based, but the tests aren't STAAR-based. We don't have a released test, so it's a guess. So when they want to bring . . . a lot of teachers and a lot of test-makers don't understand the difference between a rigorous test and a complicated test. And they're just trying to make it up as they go along, and I can understand that. It's so new, this whole STAAR test idea of everything."

Many similarities exist between the TAKS and the STAAR. For starters, 85 percent of the questions on the TAKS and 83 percent of the questions on the STAAR measured factual recognition.[39] Both exams also asked seemingly random content questions. For example, on one released TAKS, question 22 asked for the reason Thomas Paine wrote *Common Sense*, question 23 asked for the result of the Battle of Vicksburg, and question 24 asked about various treaties pertaining to the United States' westward expansion.

The STAAR exam asked similarly random content questions. Using the same question numbers on the STAAR, question 22 asked students to identify one major effect of the opening of the Erie Canal, question 23 asked students to identify the primary aim of the American Temperance Society, and question 24 asked students to identify the reason Patrick Henry opposed ratifying the US Constitution.

The main differences between the TAKS and STAAR seemed to involve the format of the new exam and the nature of the exam's reading passages. The questions on the STAAR often required students to complete charts or other graphic organizers, more difficult distractors were used, and the new exam required students to read difficult (especially in terms of reading level) excerpts from primary source documents.

The Influence of the Teachers' Knowledge and Beliefs on Their Teaching

Teachers' knowledge and beliefs also exerted power over their work. This section briefly illustrates three examples of how these teachers' knowledge and beliefs influenced their teaching. In the first example, Margaret revealed how her goals for students and her beliefs about history content shaped her teaching. Early in the study, Margaret made it clear that she would teach much of the information she had to teach as dictated by the state accountability exam even if no exam existed:

Jacob: Would you leave things out if you could, in terms of coverage?

Margaret: Yeah . . . probably . . . There's a couple of things on there [the state history curriculum] that I wouldn't stress as much . . . [but] most of it I would keep. As a matter of fact, I met with someone when I went up to the Humanities Texas, I met people who were very much involved with the Texas Legislature, and we were telling them that we don't have enough time. And one of them asked us what we would leave out, and I wrote back saying, honestly, probably none of it, except for a few minor things, like the Albany Plan of Union probably wouldn't get so much . . . the Monroe Doctrine is a big deal, but is it really? Yeah, make your point and move on; there are things I would spend more time on. Overall, you're asking a history teacher to leave out part of history. One thing connects to another. What are you going to leave out?

Jacob: So maybe some small things you would leave out.

Margaret: Maybe some small things, but overall no, everything that is in there is pretty critical that they need to know it.

This belief informed Margaret's emphasis on both facts and on what she called "why" questions. Margaret believed that knowledge of historical facts is an essential component in learning history: "Students still have to recall data. And that's not necessarily bad. There's a lot of talk in education, especially in social studies, about 'You don't need to memorize facts, data. It's stupid. It's irrelevant.' No, it's not. Because you have to have all these dates and ideas in your head so that when you come to the higher-level thinking, you can organize and know, well, that came before this, so . . . and your brain can think it through."

She also believed that the why questions sat at the core of her teaching. For Margaret, why questions help students generate critical thinking and give historical knowledge its fundamental meaning:

To me, it comes back to if your curriculum is really sound and if you're getting kids to understand the "whys." It's like when I had the kids do the difference in the fighting styles, and they understand that and the "why" behind it, then so much of it is "Oh, I get it." The triangular trade route too. Once they get that basic, fundamental difference . . . the people in New England, they're not keeping [slaves], but they're sure making money off of them, and the South is, you know, "Well they need them." Once you go into it, because it's a very complicated issue, when you try to make them understand it . . . to me it's always been about the "why."

The second example illustrates how the teachers altered prescribed curriculum guidelines based on their understanding of content and of students' needs. In this example, Mary Watson revised both the scope and the sequence of the introductory components of her sixth-grade world cultures class. The district curriculum plan prescribed separate two-week units on North America and government, followed by a week on Central America and two more weeks on South America, with a focus on current issues and little historical background. Mary felt strongly that this approach did not benefit students' learning:

All of that, can you imagine, for sixth graders? Going from North America and they barely remember that we have fifty states, maybe some of them the three branches of government—you saw today how much they remember about the three branches, and that was supposed to be last year's social studies. So I'm supposed to go from that and please have them compare at a higher level of thinking [softly laughs] our government with other forms of government.

In response, Mary combined the North America and government units into one larger unit and the separate Central and South America units into a unit she called Latin America. She changed the scope of the content to first create a historical context through which students could examine current conditions. In the unit on Latin America, Mary surveyed Mayan, Incan, and Aztec history; examined the impact of Spanish colonization; and then focused on twentieth-century Cuba. Even this revised plan moved too quickly for Mary, but it helped her to better establish deep thinking within her students. She stated that the district curriculum plan was giving teachers

> a million two-week units. Just down the road, click, click, click [makes a snapping noise with her hand] and please do them. And the order didn't even make sense at first. It wasn't geographical. All we could figure out was that we're moving from continent to continent, and please hurry through them in that order as fast as you can. But it's not a way to teach kids in any depth that's going to stick if they're just flying through the products and the forms of government; please move on to the next country. Students want stories; they want to hear shocking things and strange things and have some feeling, some emotion for how the citizens would have felt after, you know, fifty years of dictatorships in Cuba and the casinos and the nightclubs and whatever the Americans were building.

This is just one of many instances of Mary altering her prescribed curriculum scope and sequence to best serve her students. Mary shared, "I just want them to try to step in people's shoes, from wherever we're talking about, what would be reasonable and alternative ways of thinking about events. I've had to just make it fit my own way. So, I'm behind and I'm not ashamed [laughs]."

The third example demonstrates how teachers can change their teaching methods to better help their students learn. Bill Trammell had always incorporated student-centered elements such as interactive projects and cooperative learning structures into his teaching. But more teacher-centered structures, such as lectures and having students read the textbook in class and complete the review questions, comprised most of his teaching.

Midway through the study, Bill began the process of shifting his teaching away from those teacher-centered elements and toward more student-centered methods. Bill explained his efforts as working toward a move away from memorization and more toward teaching that required a deeper level of thinking and inquiry from students:

> Everybody working a job today can have the ability of accessing the Internet on their smartphones in a matter of seconds. Nobody finds it necessary to know the date of July 4, 1776, because all people have to do is know "when's the birth date of America;" they need to know keywords. That minimum level is being done at the schools. That's fine. So, how do we get to that . . . to memorize something is not as important, and doing the chapter by chapter, that's more of a memorization thing. Now, I know I'll get arguments about saying, "We still have to have a minimum." That's true, but how we accomplish that minimum doesn't necessarily have to be chapter by chapter.

These changes ranged from how Bill planned his instruction to the types of learning activities he created for his students. Ironically, perhaps, some of these changes were moves *toward* the district curriculum guidelines:

> I tried changing up some things the previous year, but I still did my own year-at-a-glance, this is what I've always covered at this time . . . I tried changing around the way I presented material and the way the students interacted with it. But this year, I did total just year-at-a-glance. And that's the feedback, the pushback you get from colleagues that, the people you mentioned, it's that they've had their system in place for so long that it's hard to change.

Because Bill had previously organized his content differently from the prescribed curriculum guidelines, following the new guidelines demanded that he rethink his established practices. He explained how his planning changed:

> I didn't do CSCOPE [the district curriculum guidelines] in the sense of using every exemplar lesson. All I did with CSCOPE was, I looked at their exemplary lessons, I looked at their year at a glance, and said these are the objectives I need to teach this six weeks, I'll do that, but I'll do it my own way. I wrote all new lesson plans for this year. I wrote all new objectives. Every day I'd have a language objective and a content objective. So they were all new this year because they had to be aligned with the year at a glance.

Bill also made significant changes to his teaching practices. By the end of the study, for example, Bill had moved away from having students routinely read the textbook aloud in class and answer review questions. Instead, he taught his students to use Thinking Maps® (a type of graphic organizer) to organize information. After much guided practice in creating and applying various concept maps, Bill was able to eventually task students with creating a thinking map that fit the content of an assigned reading.

Sometimes Bill provided the template and had students fill in relevant information, but other times, Bill had the students decide which map to use. Either way, students learned to take responsibility for making sense of the content. Additionally, during those moments when he did lecture, he stopped specifying for students how to make notes on content. Instead, he helped students learn how to actively listen and take their own notes. During these exchanges, Bill also incorporated more Socratic-type questioning into his teaching so that he was not merely telling information to students but engaging them in meaning making.

WHAT'S THE TAKEAWAY?

The preceding stories illustrate how these two broad factors, the teachers' knowledge and beliefs about teaching and the high-stakes exam, exerted power on the teachers' work. How were these factors examples of power? Because through them, the teachers influenced their teaching situations. Nowhere do these stories offer evidence of power working linearly. Sometimes power seems to just emerge, especially as the teachers make decisions about their teaching. That power was isolated and focused on solving or responding to particular needs, so it seems to appear almost haphazardly in the school landscape.

The dispersed nature of power can make it tough to untangle how the various iterations relate to each other. One might argue that power, in this story, first appeared through the teachers' knowledge and beliefs about teaching. The chapter illustrates how Margaret said she would largely teach the same content to her students, even without the high-stakes exam. And Margaret, as well as Mary and Bill, valued what she called "why" questions, and she structured her teaching to meet these self-imposed goals.

The high-stakes test, of course, also simultaneously exerted its own power. For example, in Margaret's class, the TAKS compelled her to teach to the "bubble kids," the students who were on the edge of passing. And the pacing problem caused the teachers to move much more quickly through their curriculum than they thought was pedagogically appropriate for their students. Early on, this wasn't a huge problem. Early in the study, Margaret even said, "I have found a way to do the things that I really love to do in spite of the test." Here she was referring to all of the drama, what she called "act it outs," that she used in her teaching.

But when the school failed to meet AYP, the story of school Connors had enjoyed was threatened, and the school began to impose changes that often conflicted with the teachers' time-tested practices. The pacing problem that wasn't a huge problem earlier in the study became much more significant, eventually forcing Margaret to eliminate many of those activities from her teaching because she felt that the pacing of the curriculum did not allow her enough time to engage in those activities.

Further, increases to the testing apparatus reduced the teachers' time to teach even more, as the school district implemented practices to improve students' test-taking skills and measure their learning through repeated diagnostic testing. Perhaps ironically, these teachers found that the new pacing and testing guidelines limited the amount and quality of deep and meaningful inquiry they could engage in with their students. These initiatives consumed much of the teachers' time that they could have otherwise used to develop their teaching based on their knowledge and beliefs.

Yet the teachers could still exert power over their work. You saw Mary revise her curriculum guidelines to better meet the demands of the content as well as her students' learning needs. You also saw Bill change his teaching from a more lecture-oriented, teacher-centered format to a more question-oriented, student-centered environment. Both of these changes were made *after* the AYP episode, so even with all of the added pacing and test apparatus pressures, the teachers still were able to exert power over their work.

NOTES

1. Cheryl J. Craig, "The dragon in school backyards: The influence of mandated testing on school contexts and educators' narrative knowing," *Teachers College Record* 106, no. 6 (June 2004): 1229.

2. Mary A. Barksdale and Karen F. Thomas, "What's at stake in high-stakes testing? Teachers and parents speak out," *Journal of Teacher Education* 51, no. 5 (2000): 384; K. Gaylor, *How have high school exit exams changed our schools? Some perspectives from Virginia and Maryland* (Washington, DC: Center on Educational Policy, 2005); M. Gail Jones et al., "The impact of high-stakes testing on teachers and students in North Carolina," *Phi Delta Kappan* 81, no. 3 (November 1999): 199; Mary L. Smith, "Put to the test: The effects of external testing on teachers," *Educational Researcher* 20, no. 5 (June 1991): 8; Kenneth. E. Vogler, "Impact of a high school graduation examination on social studies teachers' instructional practices," *Journal of Social Studies Research* 29, no. 2 (2005): 19; and Kenneth. E. Vogler, "Comparing the impact of accountability examinations on Mississippi and Tennessee social studies teachers' instructional practices," *Educational Assessment* 13, no. 1 (April 2008): 1.

3. Wayne Au, "Teaching under the new Taylorism: High-stakes testing and the standardization of the 21st century curriculum," *Journal of Curriculum Studies* 43, no. 1 (2011): 25.

4. Smith, "Put to the test," 10.

5. Bruce A. Vansledright and S. G. Grant, "Citizenship education and the persistent nature of classroom teaching dilemmas," *Theory and Research in Social Education* 22, no. 3 (Summer 1994): 305; John S. Wills, "Putting the squeeze on social studies: Managing teaching dilemmas in subject areas excluded from state testing," *Teachers College Record* 109, no. 8 (August 2007): 1980; and John S. Wills and Judith H. Sandholtz, "Constrained professionalism: Dilemmas of teaching in the face of test-based accountability," *Teachers College Record* 111, no. 4 (April 2009): 1065.

6. Linda Valli and Daria Buese, "The changing roles of teachers in an era of high-stakes accountability," *American Educational Research Journal* 44, no. 3 (2007): 545.

7. Margaret S. Crocco and Arthur T. Costigan, "High-stakes teaching: What's at stake for teachers (and students) in the age of accountability?" *The New Educator* 2, no. 1 (January 2006): 2.

8. Wills, "Putting the squeeze on social studies," 1980–2046; Wills and Sandholtz, "Constrained professionalism," 1065–1114.

9. Kenneth E. Vogler and David Virtue, "'Just the facts, ma'am': Teaching social studies in the era of standards and high-stakes testing," *The Social Studies* 98, no. 2 (2007): 54.

10. Wayne Au, "High-stakes testing and curricular control: A qualitative meta-synthesis," *Educational Researcher* 36, no. 5 (2007): 258; Vogler, "Impact of a high school graduation examination," 19–33; Vogler, "Comparing the impact of accountability examinations," 1–32.

11. Shawn A. Faulkner and Christopher M. Cook, "Testing vs. teaching: The perceived impact of assessment demands on middle grades instructional practices," *Research in Middle Level Education Online* 29, no. 7 (January 2006): 7–8.

12. Pamela Williamson et al., "Meeting the challenge of high-stakes testing while remaining child-centered: The representations of two urban teachers," *Childhood Education* 81, no. 4 (2005): 190.

13. Fred M. Newmann, "Higher order thinking in teaching social studies: A rationale for the assessment of classroom thoughtfulness," *Journal of Curriculum Studies* 22, no. 1 (1990): 41.

14. Wills, "Putting the squeeze on social studies," 1980–2046; Wills and Sandholtz, "Constrained professionalism," 1065–1114.

15. Patricia T. Ashton and Rodman B. Webb, *Making a difference: Teachers' sense of efficacy and student achievement* (New York: Longman, 1986); Sherri Gibson and Myron H. Dembo, "Teacher efficacy: A construct validation," *Journal of Educational Psychology* 76 (August 1984): 569; Pam L. Grossman, Suzanne M. Wilson, and Lee S Shulman, "Teachers of substance: Subject matter knowledge for teaching," in *Knowledge base for the beginning teacher*, ed. Maynard C. Reynolds (New York: Pergamon, 1989), 23; Amy R. Feiker Hollenbeck, "Beyond talking about books: Implications of the reading comprehension instruction and pedagogical beliefs of a special educator perceived as effective," *Learning Disability Quarterly* 36, no. 2 (April 2013): 112; Dona M. Kagan and Kenneth E. Smith, "Beliefs and behaviors of kindergarten teachers," *Educational Researcher* 30, no. 1 (1988): 26; Virginia Richardson et al., "The relationship between teachers' beliefs and practices in reading comprehension

instruction," *American Educational Research Journal* 28, no. 3 (1991): 559; and Tabatha D. Scharlach, "These kids just aren't motivated to read: The influence of preservice teachers' beliefs on their expectations, instruction, and evaluation of struggling readers," *Literacy research and instruction* 47, no. 1 (2008): 58.

16. Dona M. Kagan, "Implications of research on teacher belief," *Educational Psychologist* 27, no. 1 (1992): 65.

17. Ashton and Webb, *Making a difference*; Gibson and Dembo, "Teacher efficacy," 569–82; Mark D. Litt and Dennis C. Turk, "Sources of stress and dissatisfaction in experienced high school teachers," *Journal of Educational Research* 78, no. 3 (1985): 178.

18. Suzanne M. Wilson and Samuel S. Wineburg, "Peering at history through different lenses: The role of disciplinary perspectives in teaching history," *Teachers College Record* 89, no. 4 (Summer 1988): 525; Leslie C. Soodak and David M. Podell, "Teachers' thinking about difficult-to-teach students," *Journal of Educational Research* 88, no. 1 (September–October 1994): 44.

19. D. Jean Clandinin, *Classroom practice: Teacher images in action* (Philadelphia: Falmer Press, 1986); D. Jean Clandinin and F. Michael Connelly, *Teachers' professional knowledge landscapes* (New York: Teachers College Press, 1995); and Clandinin and Connelly, "Teachers' professional knowledge landscapes: Teacher stories," 24.

20. D. Jean Clandinin, "Narrative and story in teacher education," in *Teachers and teaching: From class to reflection*, ed. Tom Russell and Hugh Mumby (Philadelphia: Falmer Press, 1992), 125.

21. Clandinin and Connelly, "Teachers' professional knowledge landscapes: Teacher stories," 24.

22. Kagan, "Implications of research on teacher belief," 73.

23. Jacob W. Neumann, "Teaching to and beyond the test: The influence of mandated accountability testing on one social studies teacher's classroom," *Teachers College Record* 115, no. 6 (2013): 1.

24. Deborah P. Britzman, "Cultural myths in the making of a teacher: Biography and social structure in teacher education," *Harvard Educational Review* 56, no. 4 (December 1986): 442.

25. Kagan, "Implications of research on teacher belief," 75.

26. Fred M. Newmann, "Can depth replace coverage in the high school curriculum?" *Phi Delta Kappan* 69, no. 5 (January 1988): 345; Mary H. Metz, "Real school: A universal drama amid disparate experience," in *Education politics for a new century*, ed. Douglas E. Mitchell and Margaret E. Goertz (Bristol, PA: The Falmer Press, 1989).

27. William A. Reid, "Curriculum as institutionalized learning: Implications for theory and research," *Journal of Curriculum and Supervision* 19, no. 1 (Fall 2003): 29.

28. Newmann, "Can depth replace coverage," 345–48.

29. Reid, "Curriculum as institutionalized learning," 29–43.

30. Metz, "Real school," 85; emphasis in the original.

31. Metz, "Real school," 85.

32. Metz, "Real school," 87.

33. "STAAR Executive Summary," Texas Education Agency, published 2010, www.tea.state.tx.us/student.assessment/hb3/HB3-ExecutiveSummary.pdf

34. "STAAR to replace TAKS," Texas Education Agency, published 2010, http://www.tea.state.tx.us/index4.aspx?id=7874.

35. S. G. Grant, *Measuring history: Cases of state-level testing across the United States* (Greenwich, CT: Information Age Publishing, 2006); Vogler and Virtue, "'Just the facts, ma'am,'" 54–58.

36. Clandinin and Connelly, "Teachers' professional knowledge landscapes: Teacher stories," 24–30; Cheryl J. Craig, "Stories of schools/teacher stories: A two-part invention on the walls theme," *Curriculum Inquiry* 30, no. 1 (2000): 11.

37. Valli and Buese, "The changing roles of teachers," 519–58; Wills, ""Putting the squeeze on social studies," 1980–2046; Wills and Sandholtz, "Constrained professionalism," 1065–1114.

38. International Baccalaureate, "The IB Middle Years Programme," accessed on February 6, 2023, https://www.ibo.org/globalassets/new-structure/brochures-and-infographics/pdfs/myp-programme-brochure-en.pdf#:~:text=The%20MYP%20is%20designed%20for%20students%20aged%2011,studies%20in%20traditional%20subjects%20and%20the%20real%20world.

39. Like many states, Texas periodically updates its tests and testing procedures. The structure of the tests described here do not reflect current testing practices. For the 2022–2023 school year, the Texas Education Agency made changes such as requiring only online testing for grades 3 to 8 and capping multiple-choice test items at 75 percent of the test.

Chapter 5

The Power of "Initiatives"

Chapter 5 examines the third part of the definition of power: power comes from everywhere. So far in this book, you've read about power exerted by students and by teachers. However, power can also emerge from much smaller things, things that might be easily overlooked—in this case, school-based initiatives given by a principal or superintendent. The stories in this chapter involve all four social studies teachers at Connors: Margaret, Mary, Bill, and Orlando. What might surprise you is that these small actions exerted power just like all of the other examples examined so far in this book: they change the nature of educational situations.

Initiatives, as defined here, usually focus on how teachers teach, but they can also address other aspects of school operations. Put simply, they're directives from principals or superintendents for teachers to do something or to enact a plan of action. The initiatives presented here aim to either directly or indirectly change how teachers teach. Either way, they always seem to flow along "the conduit," usually from the "higher-ups" of school administration down into teachers' classrooms.[1]

An example of a direct initiative at Connors was the priority academic vocabulary initiative in which the administration imposed teaching practices onto teachers by telling them to make sure that students used particular words during classroom lessons. Principals wanted to be able to visit classrooms and see evidence of this vocabulary being used. An example of an indirect initiative at Connors was the instructional rounds initiative, which mandated that teachers observe their colleagues teach. Administrators hoped that teachers would learn new techniques from watching their colleagues and implement those techniques into their own teaching.

The direct approach seems to clearly be power at work; administrators simply told teachers to change their practices. But what about the indirect approach? Was this attempt at indirect change also an example of power at work? The answer must be yes. Teachers, of course, can't ignore initiatives. They have to figure out how to fit them into their work. But that's not all there is to it. This simplistic explanation seems to imply that initiatives operate in isolation, that they are things to deal with but not really things to think about, since they're supposedly isolated events, even if they sometimes come in rapid succession.

The problem with this thinking is that initiatives don't operate in isolation; they work simultaneously with everything else around them. Imagine a school as a swimming pool. Students, teachers, principals, and others come to the pool and swim around for a while each school day: learning, teaching, leading, and so forth. The water is composed of many elements—the culture of the school, people's actions within the school, notions of schooling in general, the curriculum, granular details of how the school is run, and more—what scholars have called the milieu of the school.

Also in the water are these initiatives from the central office and from principals acting on the swimmers (the students, teachers, principals, and others). Just as little bits of certain materials, such as chlorine, can create big impacts within the entire pool, initiatives, even though they might look small, can also create big impacts in the "water" of the school. And just as those materials such as chlorine must be carefully considered before being added to the pool, so too must directives and initiatives. If one adds too little chlorine, problems arise, but if one adds too much chlorine, problems also arise. The same goes with initiatives.

Principals, for example, need to be able to lead their schools, so they need to be able to implement initiatives as they see fit to make needed changes. But say that principals—or, more likely, central office administrators—get carried away with adding more and more initiatives into the "water" of the pool, trying to combat more problems. These initiatives usually don't have a short expiration date: they usually stay active in the water for a long time. We can call this the "additive" approach to school administration: trying to solve problems by doing *more*.

As more initiatives get added to the water, more keep interacting with one another, as well as with all the other materials in the pool. The practice of adding more and more initiatives reflects people's general tendency to think about solving problems through additive reasoning, as opposed to subtractive reasoning. Put differently, people usually think about doing *more* things to solve problems. Much less often do people think to do *fewer* things to solve problems.[2]

In many cases, doing *more* simply creates more problems. As one scholar puts it, "When leaders are undisciplined about piling on staff, gizmos, software, meetings, rules, training and management fads, organizations become too complicated, their people get overwhelmed and exhausted, and their resources are spread so thin that all their work suffers."[3] This chapter illustrates how this same "piling on" in business also applies to schools as teachers are asked to do more and more.

ESTABLISHING CONTEXT: A BRIEF REVIEW OF THE RESEARCH LITERATURE

The relevant research on teachers' milieu usually follows one of two lines: either the intensification of teachers' work or the structural and institutional factors that influence teachers' work. The intensification thesis began in a Marxist analysis of education as an attempt to account for the causes and effects of the growing workload teachers have faced over the past several decades.[4] Andy Hargreaves describes this line of analysis as follows: "In these accounts, teachers' work is portrayed as becoming more routinized and deskilled, more and more like the degraded work of manual workers and less and less like that of autonomous professionals trusted to exercise the power and expertise of discretionary judgment with the children. Teachers are depicted as being increasingly controlled by prescribed programs, mandated curricula, and step-by-step methods of instruction."[5]

More recent research into the intensification of teachers' work moves away from Marxist analysis and focuses on the nature and effect of the increasing numbers of tasks that teachers must deal with in their work that do not involve teaching. Examples of these intensification pressures include school district initiatives regarding student monitoring,[6] organized school reform mandates,[7] and assessment and administration demands, as well as inclusion of greater numbers of students with increased learning and emotional support needs in mainstream classrooms.[8]

The biggest impact of intensification on teachers' work is a persistent lack of time: time for curriculum planning, time for professional development, and time for personal pursuits outside of work as teachers have to work longer days or take increasing amounts of work home with them.[9] This line of research holds that the intensification of teachers' work and its concomitant time crunch leads to a narrowing of teaching practices toward efficiency and basic-skills teaching.[10]

The other line of research into teachers' milieu focuses on the structural and institutional factors that influence their work. Some of the research along this line holds that particularities of place within a teacher's milieu frame what and how teachers come to know.[11] These particularities include but are not limited to the nature of collegial relationships; the accountability context of a school, subject, or grade level; and the stories of school authorized by local school administrators.[12]

Cheryl Craig's work in particular clearly demonstrates that teachers' knowledge and beliefs are influenced by issues such as school reform efforts, collegial (or *non*collegial) relationships, effects from high-stakes testing–related issues, and local administrative decisions.[13] Indeed, she offers rich evidence of milieu-related factors that are even causing teachers to question and doubt their own knowledge and beliefs.[14]

Other research, such as Larry Cuban's work, describes how institutional patterns of schooling shape teachers' work.[15] Cuban argues that teacher-centered practices (i.e., lecturing, having students read aloud from the textbook, using worksheets, and entertaining few student questions) in secondary schools, such as the school in which this study took place, commonly result when teachers are compelled to teach too much in too short a time period to too many classes with too many students. Here's Cuban at length:

> For example, high school teachers face more than 150 students during a school day that is sliced into periods of less than an hour each; they teach five classes and prepare two or more lessons each day, which leaves them no time to grade papers at school or to meet with colleagues. Not surprisingly, they have little energy or time during or outside of class to explore ideas with students, to permit students to make errors that can then be reassessed, to listen as students try out new thoughts, question the textbook, or question the teacher's statements. Laboring under such conditions, even the best teachers are driven to make deals with students and to reduce opportunities for thinking in the classroom.[16]

In short, Cuban argues that teacher-centered practices often serve as a coping mechanism that allows teachers to efficiently teach within the structural confines imposed upon them. This does not imply, however, that institutional factors make teacher-centered practices operate to the exclusion of more student-centered practices. To the contrary, Cuban finds that teachers have employed a "hybrid" of teacher and student-centered practices in their classrooms—for example, practices such as lecture, reading aloud from textbooks, and worksheets blended with small group work, projects, and student-selected problems in science or computer labs.[17]

INITIATIVES THAT EXERTED POWER

A number of initiatives impacted teachers' work at Connors. These examples illustrate the intensification line of inquiry. During the study the teachers at Connors experienced a marked increase in the tasks they were expected to perform, thereby crowding or "intensifying" their teaching milieu.[18] These tasks created a tremendous amount of stress among the teachers. Bill

Trammell put it like this: "When they add something new, it should be a zero-sum game, meaning something should be taken away. And that's when you start to feel the stress."

According to Bill, teachers felt overwhelmed not from any one initiative in particular but from the combined effect of all of them, to the extent that they seemed to barely notice the change in high-stakes achievement exam. Around midway through the study, Texas changed exams from the TAKS to STAAR. Given all the emphasis and pressure placed on achievement test scores, one might reasonably expect teachers to evince some worry about the new exam. However, none of the teachers expressed the slightest sign of emotion regarding the change. Bill explained the nonreaction like this: "All the other things that [principals] keep adding here and there, from keeping up with TELPAS, keeping up with your special populations, things like that, just one more thing, [teachers are] not going to be . . . they're so inured to all this coming at them that 'Oh, a new test? OK.'"

These initiatives can be loosely divided into two categories: (1) indirect initiatives that focused on administrative tasks and professional development and (2) direct initiatives that changed how teachers taught. Many of the initiatives in both categories resulted from the school not meeting AYP. Others, however, seemed to result simply from the increasing bureaucratic control of schooling.[19]

Indirect Initiatives: Administration and Professional Development

Three initiatives focused on administrative duties and professional development: the homework initiative, monitoring special populations of students, and instructional rounds. The homework and monitoring initiatives were directed toward students; instructional rounds focused on teachers' teaching development. All three generated extra time, attention, and paperwork concerns for the teachers.

Homework Initiative

The school's homework initiative was designed to monitor students who consistently did not turn in homework and, thus, were at risk of failure. Teachers had to create a form that kept track of students' missed homework. Each time a student failed to turn in homework, that student completed the appropriate part of the form, which the teacher had to monitor. After a certain number of missed assignments, teachers had to call parents and possibly give the student some sort of penalty, such as on-campus "suspension." Yet once students reached this level, the paper trail started over at the beginning.

Monitoring Special Populations of Students

Tasks related to monitoring special populations of students came in several forms. Teachers of course monitor students who have labels such as 504 and need special accommodations. Students who have limited English proficiency also require special attention. For example, teachers are sometimes tasked with creating tutoring groups to deliver basic phonics instruction to these students. Another example is TELPAS. TELPAS stands for Texas English Language Proficiency Assessment System. It is designed to assess the progress that limited-English-proficient students make in learning the English language.

At Connors this applied to approximately 7 percent of the student population. Teachers were only required to collect writing samples from these students. But to reduce pressure on those students, teachers had to take class time to collect writing samples from all students. After those samples had been collected, teachers had to verify that the samples met the requirements set by the state to show language acquisition. Those samples were verified and then analyzed by a team of teachers who rated each student. Teachers were required to be certified each year in order to conduct this process.

Instructional Rounds

Instructional rounds was a school-based initiative that required teachers to observe their colleagues' teaching and submit reports on the observations. Created as a professional development mechanism, its implementation turned it into a form of teacher monitoring. Orlando Gaines described the process and his reactions to it as follows:

> Instructional rounds are a pain in the ass. Number one, they stress teachers out. It's stressful because you're turning into an administrator, which puts you in an odd position. But the time problem is my biggest complaint. You have to fill out paperwork as you do your fifteen-minute walk through. After you do your walk through, you have to sit and record on three pieces of paper what you saw, and it kind of tells you what to do. We're supposed to do two every six weeks. It takes away one conference period, either your conference period or your period with your team. In other words, it's just something else to fill out and to do. Now, is it constructive? I don't know. I think it is constructive for new teachers to be seeing other classrooms. I do like going into other classes and seeing what people do; I get ideas. So that's not a bad thing. But being forced to do it?

Mary Watson echoed Orlando's concerns:

> I just feel stretched and pulled. That and then to go evaluate my peers? Sometimes it's been, "Oh, what a great way you've questioned them."

Sometimes there's . . . I work with great people and I see some neat teaching techniques that have been nice to watch. But then to do the paperwork on that, too, and turn it in? I feel like all of our technology and all of our new ideas are not time-saving, and I don't know how much they're improving my instruction for the kids.

At Connors, instructional rounds were compounded by administrative walk-throughs of groups of principals and superintendents, up to twelve at a time, observing teachers' classrooms. These types of district-imposed walk-throughs can "height[en] anxiety levels as teachers anticipat[e] a team of individuals coming into their classrooms to make sure they [are] implementing school district expectations."[20] Orlando voiced a reaction of stress that was typical for these teachers: "What it was originally supposed to be . . . the instructional rounds, two years ago, when the superintendent came in, it started with principals doing this. You talk about stress! When three or four teachers come into your room, to me that's not stress. High stress is when you have a superintendent and twelve principals walking in."

Direct Initiatives: Initiatives Aimed at Teaching

This group of broad initiatives created far-reaching impacts on teachers' practices. Here the initiatives can be divided into three categories: what are labeled as classroom teaching initiatives, the "one iPad per child" initiative, and the International Baccalaureate program. These categories, however, held many components. The classroom teaching initiatives actually comprised at least six practices that Connors' principals expected teachers to use in their teaching. And the iPad initiative and IB program impacted their teaching in fundamental ways.

Classroom Teaching Initiatives

The teachers at Connors had been told to incorporate a variety of practices into their teaching. Administrators told teachers they would be looking for classroom evidence that teachers taught and students understood these initiatives. Four of these initiatives focused on higher-order thinking, on the four Cs (communication, cooperation, creativity, and critical thinking), on priority academic vocabulary, and on teachers' use of high-level Bloom's taxonomy questions in their teaching. The initiatives even specified how many academic words teachers had to make students use.[21]

Other initiatives focused on mandatory professional development. For example, Connors's principal secured a subscription to PD 360, a web-based service through which teachers were assigned to watch selections of online videos with questions to be answered and that was trackable by the administration, complete with various topics to be viewed and reflected upon by specified deadlines.

Yet another initiative, what might be called the questioning initiative, required teachers to use their conference periods to observe each other teach and note the language that teachers used in posing questions to their students. Teachers wrote the phrasing of the questions they heard on Post-it notes and then placed those Post-its on a large chart that was affixed to a wall in the teachers' lounge and organized according to Bloom's taxonomy. The teachers were then supposed to collaborate in determining how to change the phrasing of their questions to generate higher-order thinking.

"One iPad per Child" Initiative

Early in the study, the school district that Connors is in began implementing a massive initiative informally called "one iPad per child." Through this initiative each student in the school district, some twenty-five thousand students, was given a new iPad for the school year. Students were instructed to bring these devices to school, and teachers were expected to incorporate them into their teaching. However, little to no formal, substantive training was given to students on how to use the iPads or to teachers on how to teach with them. This initiative created immense challenges for the teachers. Bill Trammell explained some of these challenges:

> *Bill:* [The] iPads have changed everything. When it comes to a lot of day-to-day things . . . if you've been a teacher for a long time, you're used to certain teaching modes, and now you're having to deal with things that you never had to deal with before, on the distraction level, on the discipline level. Just the fact that these kids don't know how to use them effectively. Some teachers are banning iPads from their classrooms, some aren't using it effectively, and some are having real discipline issues. Other teachers, I can speak for myself, I'm constantly redirecting when I didn't have to before. The kids, it's so new to them that it's a huge disruption. It's a huge disruption.
>
> *Jacob:* It hasn't become a teaching tool yet, campus wide?
>
> *Bill:* Not yet. It can be. There are huge possibilities, but it requires a lot of teachers to change their ideas about things and the way they run things. And a lot of teachers don't want to do that. I can understand why, because if you've been doing it a certain way and you've always had success that way, then why change?

The school district encouraged teachers to use the iPads in their teaching but neglected to offer substantive training on how to do so. As Orlando put it,

"The iPads are not a bad thing. But just throwing them at students and teachers is not a great thing." Mary Watson shared some of her concerns about using the iPads: "I'm kind of at a loss, thinking what the iPad can do, and do I really want students emailing me with homework? I like having something where students can show what they've learned, where they can study, where I can say, 'Turn to this section and page so that we're ready for the exam.' I'm wanting to connect the two. Maybe I'm the dinosaur here." Here Mary contemplated the tension between her tried-and-tested paper-and-pencil approach to notetaking and teaching and the, at the time, unknown possibilities of that new tool.

The teachers also found that the iPads ironically, at least in those early stages, seemed to reduce the quality and depth of thought in students' research, which complicated how teachers framed and guided research projects. Mary Watson explained this phenomenon: "I'm frustrated about reading. Kids don't read today. They will have a lot of discussion about the pictures that they see, but they won't read the captions or articles that go with it. Having the images at the fingertips of the kids fascinates me. But the effort put into the research is rather low quality in most cases."

The teachers found that instead of reading, summarizing, and analyzing information, students simply copied and pasted, so they learned little. This presented another challenge to their teaching, as the teachers were forced to rethink how they conceptualized research to promote learning.

International Baccalaureate (IB)

At the time of the study, Connors was an IB (International Baccalaureate) school, which could be considered a long-term initiative. The "sacred story" of the IB program, the story told by school district officials that teachers challenge at their peril, was that IB increased the rigor and quality of learning for all students. But the secret "teacher stories," the stories that teachers told amongst like-minded colleagues, revealed a more complicated relationship with IB.[22] For these teachers, IB reflected pedagogical approaches that they already took in their classroom but that required more paperwork.

For example, Orlando Gaines claimed, "I love the school. I love teaching. I just don't love IB. The IB stuff we were doing anyway. We were doing all the higher-level, worldly things without having the paperwork." For these teachers, the main influence of IB was the paperwork and external oversight. Orlando claimed, "I think if you talk to any teacher, it's insane the amount of paperwork for IB." According to Orlando,

> IB has been a major wrench. And now it's not four units for us; it's going to be six. Which means every six weeks [grading period the teachers must implement

an IB unit with their students]. One problem with our planning is that you think you have a good IB unit, and we have one of our visits from one of the consultants, we have a consultant come in, and she looks at your unit and she shoots it down. Some of our units could be changed, but do you have the energy to spend all this time working on the unit?

In the following interview excerpt, Mary Watson explained the IB paperwork burden:

Jacob: It sounds like the biggest pressure, the biggest influence is the pacing issue.

Mary: That's mine.

Jacob: Yeah, that's what it sounds like. And it's compounded with IB requirements and paperwork requirements. Maybe it's not . . . is it the paperwork involved?

Mary: That's the worst part of the IB.

Jacob: The paperwork?

Mary: Yes.

Jacob: I've been in a couple of meetings where y'all were going through the checklists, and I've talked with Margaret about rubrics for rubrics.

Mary: Yes.

Jacob: That's an interesting phrase: a rubric for a rubric.

Mary: We need to evaluate our rubrics so we can see if it is an appropriate rubric to evaluate their work, yes [laughing softly].

Beyond paperwork, IB complicates teachers' grading systems, their conceptualizations of rigor, and their instructional planning. Let me quote at length an interview excerpt with Bill Trammell as he explained the influence of the IB grading system.

Bill: When they add something new, it should be a zero-sum game, meaning something should be taken away. And that's when you start to feel the stress, when you start to feel the—like to give you an example with the IB, and this is something that I have a real issue with, because it is a conversion process and that adds another level of work. IB has a totally separate assessment system, and they have a certain scale that you have to grade on, and they're changing this, they're changing this to an eight-point scale for humanities. Before, what we did this year, three of them had an eight-point scale . . . no, one of them had an eight-point scale; the three others had a one-to-ten-point scale. The thing is that a ten-point scale does not directly equate [to] one is a ten, two is a twenty, it doesn't, to the point of we have to figure out . . . it's kind of like serving two masters. We keep separate IB assessment criteria, and then we have to convert that to a district grade, which is on the zero-to-a-hundred-point scale.

Jacob: So the eight-point scale to a hundred . . .

Bill: Right. Or the ten-point scale to a hundred, and you would think, 'Oh, well, one would be a ten, ten would be a hundred.' No, it doesn't work like that. If you read the criteria, some of the stuff that we would assign in a zero to a hundred-point scale, a four could be a seventy-five . . . or a three, even. So, we have to figure these kinds of things out when we grade, and it converts, we want to make sure that if a kid shows some effort, it's not going to be a forty or a ten or a twenty. . . . That's just one example of how we have to take this grading scale and make this square fit into a circle. And that just adds another level of time and effort. Then when we actually grade, we go through the IB side, and then we say, "OK, how do we convert it in a fair manner?"

Jacob: You have to think of both things at the same time.

Bill: Exactly. And it's unfair to say, OK . . . to be truly IB you need to have this framework in your mind when you're grading, and then in the back of our minds, we're going, "Yeah, but this is a test grade. This is something that we worked on for so long, so I'm going to have to put this in my gradebook and have that fit into all the other grades that we do for the regular district grade." So that just right there is an example of how we added the IB component, but we really didn't take anything away.

WHAT'S THE TAKEAWAY?

In chapter 4 teachers exerted power productively to shape teaching situations to fit their specific and contextual needs. The examples in this chapter, however, show teachers *feeling* the effects of power through these various indirect and direct initiatives. Most of their feelings were negative, often revealing considerable amounts of stress. Why focus on teachers' negative feelings when making the case that power comes from everywhere? Because while it's the big stuff that usually gets all the attention—for example, broad reform efforts, state curriculum changes, and high-stakes testing revisions—it's the little stuff that teachers often feel the most.

The main point here comes from the intensification literature: it's not that any one of these initiatives in isolation overwhelms teachers, even though several by themselves caused teachers to feel significant stress, such as the IB program and the introduction of iPads. Instead, it's the cumulative effect that wore on teachers the most: it's all of the initiatives together in addition to all of their teaching concerns that make teachers "feel stretched and pulled," as Mary Watson put it.

Because power comes from everywhere, teachers can exert it to shape their teaching. But they can also feel it from everywhere, and they tend to feel it a lot. As Bill Trammell put it, "When a lot of my colleagues say, 'Things have changed,' it's because all these things hit at once." Here Bill was referring to increasing pacing problem time constraints, a further loss of teaching time due to the testing apparatus, the change in the high-stakes accountability exam, an intensified milieu, the introduction of iPads, and increased requirements in the IB program.

Consider how two of these initiatives compounded with other factors to "stretch and pull" teachers: the introduction of iPads and the IB program. The iPad initiative forced many teachers to adapt their teaching by integrating this new technology into their teaching largely on their own; no substantive training was initially offered for how to use them. This was problematic on multiple levels. Many teachers had little experience with iPads, so even learning basic functions posed difficulties, let alone advanced pedagogical uses with students. Further, the intensified milieu reduced the amount of time and energy the teachers had to learn to use the iPads.

The IB program also created a range of conflicts. Perhaps most importantly, teachers felt pulled in two directions: by the speed required by the district curriculum plan and testing schedule and by the depth of study required by the IB program. One went fast and the other went slow, creating an almost irreconcilable tension. Teachers felt this tension throughout the year as they tried to navigate the limitations presented by the pacing problem and the testing apparatus while also fulfilling the spirit and requirements of the IB program. Indeed, years into the study, the teachers were still learning how to equitably satisfy these two competing demands.

Plus, the planning and paperwork demands of the IB program competed for teachers' time with elements within the teachers' milieu such as instructional rounds, the homework initiative, and teaching-related initiatives. Thus, while the IB program consumed considerable amounts of teachers' time and energy, teachers might have had more time to devote to IB if they were not also pressed by all of the other demands within their milieu.

Further, the teachers' intensified milieu combined with the school's failure to meet AYP to create even more testing and curriculum changes. Perhaps ironically, the teachers found that the new pacing and testing guidelines limited the amount and quality of deep and meaningful inquiry they could engage in with their students. The failure to meet AYP intensified the teachers' milieu as local administrators instituted a number of initiatives presumably designed to improve test scores. These initiatives, however, consumed much of the teachers' time that they could otherwise have used to develop their teaching.

The experience of these teachers at Connors, just like many of the teachers studied throughout the intensification literature, illustrates how *addition* in the attempt to address problems can actually create problems: adding programs, adding tasks, adding procedures, adding paperwork. One scholar, Leidy Klotz, a professor of engineering, architecture, and business at the University of Virginia, writes that when "we default to adding requirements, too many rules and too much red tape can distract from the behavior we're really hoping for."[23]

Klotz doesn't argue against adding. He doesn't claim that people should never create new programs, procedures, rules, or products. Instead, he encourages people and organizations to rethink the value of *subtraction*. Subtraction, in this context, means paring down, getting rid of what isn't working or useful, and eliminating waste and unnecessary redundancy. Klotz advocates thinking about adding and subtracting simultaneously to improve efficiency and quality. Indeed, he claims, "Whether we think add *or* subtract or add *and* subtract is a key difference in how people approach change."[24]

People seem hardwired to add. Klotz notes, "To decide that less is more, we need to see it as an option in the first place, and often we don't."[25] Klotz's research, discussed in his book *Subtract: The Untapped Science of Less*, shows how people need to be cued to consider removing things to solve problems. But people never need to be cued to add things. From making Lego structures sturdier to making diagrams symmetrical to improving holes on a miniature golf course, people consistently and almost without fail add elements to tasks when trying to solve problems—and almost never think to remove elements.

For example, Klotz asked people to make simple images symmetrical (such as figure 1). Almost always, people thought to add a shaded block (such as figure 2). But they almost never thought to remove a shaded block (such as figure 3). In this case, it appears to require equal amounts of work to change the blocks in figures 2 and 3: change one square. Klotz's research explores many permutations of experiments like this, examining a range of variables and the conditions under which people thought—or didn't think—to subtract to solve problems.

It matters little, of course, if people add or subtract a block in a simple exercise to make the image symmetrical. But adding without also subtracting can have major consequences in real life. Klotz makes this connection vividly: "We humans neglect an incredibly powerful option; we don't subtract. We pile on to-dos but don't consider stop-doings. We create incentives for high performance but don't get rid of obstacles to our goals. We draft new laws without abolishing outdated legislation. Whether we're seeking better behavior from our kids or designing new initiatives at work, we systematically opt for more over less."[26]

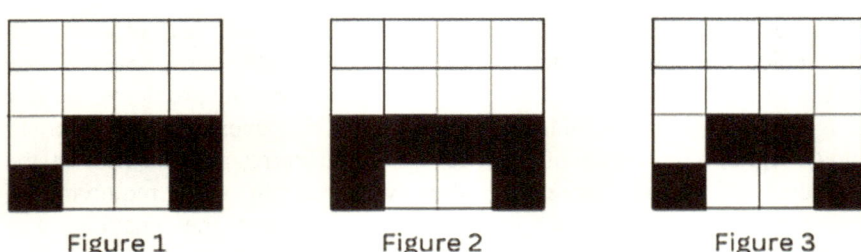

Figure 5.1. Klotz Exercise. *Source*: Leidy Klotz.

The teachers at Connors felt the power of initiatives—specifically the *addition* of initiatives. It wasn't just, say, instructional rounds with its accompanying time and paperwork demands. It was also the homework initiative *and* the IB program *and* having to learn to teach with iPads *and* the four Cs *and* PD 360 *and* the questioning initiative *and* just teaching their classes. From the teachers' perspective, nobody ever stopped to think, "Is it possible to give teachers too much?" When are they supposed to have time to think? To just think? Because thinking takes uninterrupted time, something the teachers never had.

Even worse, the teachers never saw or knew of initiatives getting reviewed. They saw initiatives get systematically implemented, but they never knew evidence of initiatives getting evaluated for efficacy or even usefulness. As a result, they never knew if initiatives actually worked. Like in Klotz's research, more initiatives just kept getting added to the metaphorical swimming pool that was the school, where they kept floating around, causing trouble for the swimmers (who are the teachers in this metaphor). And once they were added, none ever seemed to be taken away.

Seen through this lens of adding and subtracting, initiatives might be said to hold a positive productive power or a negative hindering power—or both, depending on the time and circumstance. By themselves, initiatives such as instructional rounds or the questioning initiative can provide positive value to the school. Teachers benefit by gaining new teaching ideas and learning new questioning and inquiry strategies. But initiatives become burdensome when the time, paperwork, and attention required make them feel like a chore instead of a benefit.

Subtracting can help. In the case of Connors, maybe teachers didn't also need to fill out paperwork to document their instructional rounds. Maybe teachers could have been trusted to learn on their own without the added surveillance of paperwork. Maybe one teaching initiative at a time could have been implemented, along with built-in evaluation procedures to help teachers and principals determine their effectiveness—before more teaching initiatives were implemented. Maybe school leaders could have deliberated with teachers on how to seamlessly balance IB demands with scope and sequence pacing.

Of course, it's easy to second guess school administrators' decisions. They likely had good reasons for their actions. Perhaps they wanted to get a sense of teachers' experiences during their instructional rounds. Or perhaps failing to meet AYP spurred a sense of urgency to try many initiatives in a short span. But the truth remains about the additive effect of the initiatives, as well as the truth about a lack of subtracting.

Two takeaways, then, seem most appropriate. First, addition without subtraction hurts schools just as it hurts other fields. The intensification literature as well as the experiences of these teachers at Connors clearly support this. Second, subtraction, even though it might feel uncomfortable and perhaps even risky, deserves thought. Because power comes from everywhere, having too many initiatives, each emanating their own power, causes problems. School leaders should keep this in mind as they diligently and continually strive to improve their schools and the learning experiences of their students.

NOTES

1. Clandinin and Connelly, "Teachers' professional knowledge landscapes: Teacher stories," 24–30.

2. Gabrielle S. Adams et al., "People systematically overlook subtractive changes," *Nature* 592 (April 2021): 258–61.

3. Robert I. Sutton, "Why bosses should ask employers to do less—not more," *Wall Street Journal*, September, 25, 2022, https://www.wsj.com/articles/bosses-staff-employees-less-work-11663790432?mod=Searchresults_pos1&page=1.

4. Michael W. Apple, *Teachers and texts: A political economy of class and gender relations in education* (London: Routledge, 1986); Michael W. Apple and Susan Jungck, "You don't have to be a teacher to teach this unit: Teaching, technology, and control in the classroom," in *Understanding teacher development*, ed. Andy Hargreaves and Michael G. Fullan (London: Cassell, 1996) 20–44; Kathleen Densmore, "Professionalism, proletarianization, and teachers' work," in *Critical studies in teacher education*, ed. Thomas Popkewitz (London: Falmer Press, 1987), 130–60; and Sarfatti Larson, "Proletarianization and educated labor," *Theory and Society* 9, no. 1 (January 1980): 131–75.

5. Andy Hargreaves, "Time and teachers' work: An analysis of the intensification thesis," *Teachers College Record* 94, no. 1 (1992): 87–88.

6. Katrijn Ballet and Geert Kelchtermans, "Struggling with workload: Primary teachers' experience of intensification," *Teaching and Teacher Education* 25, no. 8 (November 2009): 1150–57.

7. Cheryl J. Craig, "The relationship between and among teachers' narrative knowledge, communities of knowing, and school reform: A case of 'The Monkey's Paw,'"

Curriculum Inquiry 31, no. 3 (2001): 303; Craig, "Butterfly under a pin," 90; Craig, "Coming to know in the 'eye of the storm,'" 25; and Mary M. Kennedy, *Inside teaching: How classroom life undermines reform* (Cambridge, MA: Harvard University Press, 2005).

8. Chris Easthope and Gary Easthope, "Intensification, extension, and complexity of teachers' workload," *British Journal of Sociology of Education* 21, no. 1 (March 2000): 43; Hargreaves, "Time and teachers' work," 87–108; and Valli and Buese, "The changing roles of teachers," 519.

9. Katrijn Ballet, Geert Kelchtermans, and John Loughran, "Beyond intensification towards a scholarship of practice: Analysing changes in teachers' work lives," *Teachers and Teaching: Theory and Practice* 12, no. 2 (2006): 209; R. J. Campbell and S. R. Neill, *Primary teachers at work* (London: Routledge, 1994); Andrew Gitlin, "Bounding teacher decision making: The threat of intensification," *Educational Policy* 15, no. 2 (May 2001): 227; and Andy Hargreaves, *Changing teachers, changing times: Teachers' work and culture in the postmodern age* (New York: Teachers College Press, 1994).

10. Ballet and Kelchtermans, "Struggling with workload," 1150–57; Valli and Buese, "The changing roles of teachers," 519–58.

11. Cheryl J. Craig, "The influence of context on one teacher's interpretive knowledge of team teaching," *Teaching and Teacher Education* 14, no. 4 (1998): 371.

12. Clandinin and Connelly, "Teachers' professional knowledge landscapes: Teacher stories," 24–30; and Craig, "Stories of schools/teacher stories," 11.

13. Craig, "The relationship between and among teachers' narrative knowledge," 303–31; Craig, "Butterfly under a pin," 90–101; Craig, "Coming to know," 25–38; and Kennedy, *Inside teaching*.

14. Craig, "The dragon in school backyards," 1229.

15. Larry Cuban, "Persistent instruction: The high school classroom," *Phi Delta Kappan* 64, no. 2, (October 1982): 113; Larry Cuban, "Persistent instruction: Another look at constancy in the classroom," *Phi Delta Kappan* 68, no. 1 (September 1986): 7; and Larry Cuban, "The lure of curricular reform and its pitiful history," *Phi Delta Kappan* 75, no. 2 (October 1993): 182.

16. Cuban, "Persistent instruction: Another look," 10.

17. Larry Cuban, "Hugging the middle: Teaching in an era of testing and accountability, 1980–2005," *Education Policy Analysis Archives* 15, no. 1 (January 2007): 1.

18. Valli and Buese, "The changing roles of teachers," 519–58.

19. Apple, *Teachers and texts*.

20. Valli and Buese, "The changing roles of teachers," 544.

21. The school administration implemented four different types of teaching initiatives:

> H.E.A.T. (higher order thinking, engagement, application to the real world, and technological proficiency). Teachers were expected to incorporate these strategies into their lessons, and administrators expected students to be able to explain it as well.

Teachers had to frequently remind students about the four Cs—communication, cooperation, creativity, and critical thinking. Teachers had to articulate how they incorporated the four Cs into their lessons.

Teachers had to directly teach priority academic vocabulary—five words per week that administrators expected to see during walk-throughs.

Teachers had to use the question wheel, which was simply an adaptation of Bloom's taxonomy that was purchased by administrators to help teachers identify and generate higher-order questions in class activities.

22. Clandinin and Connelly, *Teachers' professional knowledge landscapes*.

23. Leidy Klotz, *Subtract: The untapped science of less* (New York: Flatiron Books, 2021), 13.

24. Klotz, *Subtract*, 105.

25. Klotz, *Subtract*, 49.

26. Klotz, *Subtract*, 247.

Chapter 6

The Problem of Consequences

Chapter 6 examines the final part of the definition of power: power acts like a web. School leaders have to try to predict the future. Lots of the decisions they make, perhaps most of them, hinge on these predictions: from the number of lunches the cafeteria will provide to the impact of a school homework policy to the hiring of new staff. Oftentimes, substantial money, time, and effort are at stake: nobody wants to waste food, everyone should want to discern the most useful and appropriate function of homework, and it's always bad to hire the wrong staff.

Yet people are bad at predicting the future. Part of the problem, as the philosopher Henri Bergson sees it, is that "of the future, only that is foreseen which is like the past or can be made up again with elements like those of the past."[1] It's a fraught endeavor, of course, trying to identify those elements of the present that might resemble events in the future. So much gets in the way: hopes, fears, knowledge, and more. This happens so much that predicting the future oftentimes boils down to a type of guesswork because the future always "has some degree of novelty which we cannot completely predict from our previous experience."[2]

Another part of the problem is rose-colored glasses. Put simply, people see what they want to see. Thus, predictions of the future often have a "wish-fulfilling" character.[3] If people want something to happen, they will more likely believe that it will happen.[4] The converse also holds true: people are much less likely to predict—or even think of—less desirable events.[5] This aligns with common sense: as one psychologist puts it, those who are the beneficiaries of an existing state of affairs are extremely unlikely to predict its end.[6]

Two brief examples illustrate these phenomena: In a study lasting from 1956 to 1962, a psychologist in South Africa asked 436 high school and college students to write essays about their predictions for the future. While almost all students wrote about apartheid, 80 percent of Black students predicted that apartheid would end, but only 4 percent of White students predicted that it would end. In the second example, during the strong economy of 2007, almost no economists predicted a recession or significant economic downturn for the following year—which was the 2008 housing market collapse![7]

A third part of the problem of future predictions is what's called *confirmation bias*, which is sometimes oversimplified to mean selecting evidence that supports what you already believe. But this proposition is not so simple. For example, the line is not clear between consciously and purposefully gathering evidence—cherry-picking, if you will—to support a case and a more subconscious, non-overt propensity to be attracted toward facts that align with one's beliefs. And it's "less apparent why people should be partial in their uses of evidence when they are indifferent to the answer to a question in hand."[8]

Compounding all of this is the tendency for people not just to focus on what most benefits them but also for people to become unrealistically optimistic about their own futures.[9] One definition of the future illustrates such optimism: "That [it is a] period of time in which our affairs prosper, our friends are true, and our happiness is assured."[10] Oh, if only one could know that to be true—how glorious! Alas, as most people seem to understand, things happen. Or as a religious person might put it, people plan and God laughs.

So predicting the future is difficult in any situation. Within schools, you can add one more complicating factor: an incomplete understanding of the web of power. It's common to think that power—and its consequences—only rolls downhill, from the more powerful onto the less powerful. For example, people often think that principals and other educators in supervisory positions are immune to the effects of power. Indeed, people often think that power *comes from* such positions. But that's not the way power works in schools. Instead, power acts like a web, and since webs are sticky, they impact everyone, so everybody can feel their consequences.

This web of power, what Foucault calls a "network of power relations," refers to the back-and-forth movement and exchange of power between free people.[11] Foucault sees power relations as being rooted deeply within societies, not as "a supplementary structure over and above society whose radical effacement one could perhaps dream of."[12] In other words, there's no avoiding them. If a society is free even a little bit, people can act. If they can act, they can act with or against other people's actions, exerting power on those actions and thus creating the web of power.

This chapter analyzes three stories that illustrate this web of power, the consequences it can create, and the connections to future predictions in schools. In doing so, the chapter completes the analysis trajectory that began in chapter 3: first the students, followed by teachers, then initiatives, and now educators in supervisory roles. These stories come from Tomas Gracia, Hector Resendez, and Lionel Avila. One works in a large urban school district (over eighty thousand students), one works in a medium-sized urban district (forty thousand to sixty thousand students), and the third works in a small urban district (twenty thousand to thirty-five thousand students).[13]

In none of these stories does one person act as a decision maker whose decisions are final with no pushback, ramifications, or other nonintended effects. This is because "power relations are rooted in the whole network of the social."[14] In society, this social complexity component of power seems obvious. Of course, people work from their own agendas: people act and other people act in response. Where freedom exists, people can act on the actions of others, such as stopping, slowing, reversing, diminishing, or enlarging other people's actions. It doesn't happen accidentally, because people make choices regarding their actions.

For some reason, though, people often seem to forget that power also works like this inside schools. Just as, say, school initiatives exert unintended consequences, so do the actions of principals, instructional specialists, and other educational leaders. School leaders should remain vigilant as to these consequences. Too often, however, leaders just barrel through without carefully hypothesizing both foreseen *and unforeseen* effects. This chapter illustrates the problems of rushing—or not rushing through. Two of the leaders had to handle the consequences of *other* people barreling through, and the third demonstrates the wisdom of moving cautiously.

THREE EVERYDAY STORIES THAT ILLUSTRATE THE WEB OF POWER IN SCHOOLS

The following stories illustrate three practical, everyday examples of power in schools: changing testing procedures within a dual-language program, canceling a high school career and technical education (CTE) class because of low enrollment, and deciding whether or not to fire a low-performing teacher. All three stories demonstrate what might colloquially be called the problem of consequences—or, more accurately, the problem of *unintended* consequences. A thorough understanding of the web of power is crucial to running schools since leaders constantly have to make decisions based on future predictions—which are fraught with problems in part because of the web of power.

The problems within these three stories had different resolutions. In the dual-language problem, the resolution was unknown. In the CTE problem, negative effects were felt but mitigated for the future. In the low-performing teacher problem, negative effects were avoided. The point in all three cases is that the problems themselves illustrate the web of power more effectively than do the nature of the resolutions. The problems show the "tug" between different points within the web of power. They show exchanges within the web and that, sometimes, the reactions can be predicted, but not always, which means people need to be mindful and aware.

A quick note about the participants. Among them, as of this writing, they have forty-eight years of total experience in schools: Hector Resendez, a dual-language instructional specialist, has eighteen years; Lionel Avila, an elementary school principal, has thirteen years; and Tomas Gracia, a high school principal, has seventeen years. They work in public school districts of different sizes and in different parts of Texas. All other details about them will be kept anonymous to protect their confidentiality.

Story No. 1: Changing Testing Procedures in a Dual-Language Program

The first story shows an indifference to power. Well, that's not quite right. The word *indifference* suggests awareness of a thing but not a caring about the thing. In this example the main player seems unaware of the existence of power but also seems simultaneously aware of her own power to change a situation. Perhaps power at the service of expediency puts it best. The context of the story is testing procedures in a two-way dual-language program, a form of bilingual education. The pivotal action in the story was motivated by a desire to solve a problem and was either not aware of or not caring about the problems this action would create.

The Context

But first, why are the testing procedures for dual-language programs something to worry about? A little context about dual-language programs can provide some insight. Languages originally thrived in early polyglot America. In the early nineteenth century, people organized schools and provided for instruction in a wide variety of languages, including German, Dutch, French, Spanish, Norwegian, Czech, Polish, Italian, and Cherokee, as well as English. Further, various states and territories have recognized the need for bilingual education since the nineteenth century, such as when Ohio authorized German-English instruction in 1839.

However, from the late 1800s through the 1920s, several factors combined to shift public thinking away from language multiplicity and toward prioritizing English. In the late 1800s, the scale of immigration increased, especially from Southern and Eastern Europe. This concentration of different languages, notably in crowded East Coast cities such as Philadelphia and Baltimore, stimulated a goal of Americanizing recent immigrants to bolster public cohesiveness—to make a stronger public. When World War I came in 1914, this push increased as distrust of Germany and German immigrants grew, which accentuated Americanizing efforts.

Beginning in the 1920s, court cases began to chip away at English-only efforts. For example, in 1924, *Meyer v. Nebraska* affirmed parents' rights to choose the language for their children's schooling within private schools. In 1948 *Delgado v. Bastrop ISD of Bastrop County* ruled against segregating Spanish-speaking students on the basis of language. In 1971, in *Lau v. Nichols*, the US Supreme Court made bilingual education compulsory for school districts across the country. The court held that a lack of supplementary language instruction violated limited English proficient (LEP) students' rights under the Civil Rights Act of 1964.

At the federal level, bilingual education has existed since at least 1967, with the passage of the Bilingual Education Act, which was Title VII of the Elementary and Secondary Education Amendments of 1967. This was the first federal legislation that recognized the needs of LEP students. The act awarded federal funding in the form of competitive grants to school districts to create innovative programs that help LEP students. This act was limited: it was voluntary and only applied to students ages three to eight. But it signaled new opportunities for bilingual education and a new focus on LEP students' needs.

Nowadays, there are two main types of bilingual education programs: a maintenance program and a transitional program. In maintenance programs students learn a new language (designated as L2) while maintaining and developing their native language (L1). In transitional programs students receive instruction in their native language (L1) while they learn the new language (L2). When students achieve enough proficiency in the L2, all of their instruction is moved to the new language.

Dual-language programs are a type of maintenance program. Dual-language programs are usually either *one-way* or *two-way* programs. In one-way programs, the students will share the same native language and are learning the same new language, such as a class of native Spanish speakers who are all learning English. In a two-way program, half of the students are native speakers in one language (say, Spanish), and the other half are native speakers in another language (say, English). In this case, the native Spanish speakers are learning English while the native English speakers are learning Spanish, all in the same classroom together.

Dual-language programs, at least in Texas, only exist in elementary schools. These programs divide the time students spend in each language usually from a 90/10 split to a 50/50 split (or somewhere in between). For example, first graders in a one-way program have a 90/10 split, which means that they receive 90 percent of instruction in their L1 and 10 percent in their L2. They would progress to a 50/50 split by fifth grade. In an English/Spanish dual-language program, language is by divided by content, such as math in English, science and social studies in Spanish, and language arts being divided between the two languages.

This language division is absolute for teachers. While students might talk amongst themselves in whichever language they choose, teachers must stick to the particular language at hand—if Spanish, then Spanish; if English, then English. This means that if teachers are teaching in, say, English, and a Spanish L1 student asks for help, the teachers must provide that help in English and not explain anything in Spanish, even if the student doesn't fully understand the English. Thus, these programs are usually called dual-language immersion. They're a sort of revolving immersion in that students are either fully immersed in one language or the other.

In Texas how students in two-way, English/Spanish dual-language programs are assessed under STAAR depends on the subject, on the students' fluency with English, and on decisions made by the teacher and the language proficiency assessment committee (LPAC).[15] Commonly in Texas, math is tested in English, and science is tested in Spanish. It's the reading test that will vary due to the grade level and to students' language fluency.[16] Schools typically begin planning in the fall for which language students will test in the spring.

The LPAC committee plays a crucial role in determining the language for testing. It is composed of a campus administrator, a certified bilingual teacher, and a parent of a dual-language student. This committee typically looks at three indicators in assessing the testing language: students' scores on benchmark and previous STAAR reading exams, students' scores on the Texas English Language Proficiency Assessment System (TELPAS; an assessment of English academic proficiency), and teacher input. In Texas this committee is supposed to have the final decision on language use for testing.

In many school districts, as well as in Hector's school district, the LPAC looks at the combination of evidence and makes a testing decision in late October or early November (STAAR is administered in mid to late April). The school then aims instruction toward the particular language of testing. The school accomplishes this through the percentage of English or Spanish used for instruction and through the types of language arts materials used.

The LPAC decision can't be ignored. If a school fails to follow that decision, it will receive what's called an *irregularity* from TEA (the Texas Education Agency) at the time of testing. TEA takes irregularities seriously. Schools must explain to TEA why irregularities occurred. If a school receives too many irregularities, the school (and the school district) can be put on probation or even taken over by the state. Individual school personnel can also face penalties. If conditions are deemed severe enough, TEA can and will revoke educators' teaching and principalship certifications. So schools have every incentive to avoid irregularities.

The Problem

When Hector worked as a dual-language instructional specialist, he visited elementary schools across his district. He talked about a tension between two types of fidelity: fidelity to the dual-language program and fidelity to test scores on STAAR. The goal of a dual-language program is for students to become bilingual, biliterate, and bicultural. This requires fidelity to the program. Families sign up for this program because these goals are meaningful to them, and the school district advertises its dual-language program to the community. Hector was dismayed, then, when he repeatedly saw a lack of fidelity to the tenets and practices of the program.

A main example, Hector recalled, was when a campus principal would change a student's language for testing. This usually applied to a fifth grader who was slated to take the reading STAAR in Spanish, and the principal made that student test in English (the reverse could also exist, of course, in which a principal makes a student test in Spanish instead of English). Savvy principals can convene the LPAC committee to change the testing language, which avoids an irregularity. How, though, can principals compel such a change, even shortly before testing? Principals can exert lots of power.

But why would a principal make such a change, especially when the LPAC likely made a considered decision back in the fall? The answer is test scores. Hector put the rationale like this: "The principals were deciding what language they were testing on, and it didn't matter if we marketed the district as worried about creating bilingual, biliterate, bicultural students. But internally, there was enough evidence that it didn't really matter if the student did learn Spanish or if they were exited as an English learner. At the end of the day, what mattered was if they passed STAAR."

Hector didn't know the principals' exact reasoning, of course. There's no way he could. But two possible explanations stand out. They involve students' immediate and also future chances of passing STAAR. Principals need students to pass, so perhaps a principal, after reviewing dual-language students' records, decides a student has a greater chance of passing STAAR reading in the language *not* designated for testing.

Take a Spanish L1 fifth grader who has passed reading in Spanish in third and fourth grades; who scored highly on TELPAS; and who, as a result, was scheduled to test reading in English. Or take the opposite: an English L1 fifth grader who the LPAC decided was ready to test reading in Spanish. All along, teachers would have been preparing those students to test in the designated language. But the perusing principal could easily and, according to Hector, frequently make those students test in the other language just because it seemed like the students might be more likely to pass in their L1 language instead of the language they were learning.

A further justification that Hector heard principals make for those decisions is that since dual language ends in fifth grade and all students in sixth grade take STAAR in English, fifth graders might as well test in English since they'll test in English the next year. This logic doesn't help present passing chances, but it ostensibly helps justify changing students' dual language program with the argued benefit of preparing them for future testing practices. Hector explained that "if students are tested in English, the instruction they receive in fifth grade will benefit the middle school teachers and that whole ecosystem."

Story No. 2: Canceling a High School CTE Class Because of Low Enrollment

The second story demonstrates how the web of power can work in hidden ways, even from a principal's eyes, and overturn a reasonable decision that a high school principal had to make. In this example Tomas followed his school district guidelines and made a decision at the beginning of the school year to cancel a class due to low enrollment. A few weeks later, however, he was notified by his assistant superintendent to reinstate the class, even though its enrollment was below district minimums. What was the reason? The power working behind the scenes.

The class in question in this story was a career and technical education (CTE) class. These classes used to be known as vocational classes. CTE classes are different from the regular high school curriculum. They're funded differently. They're evaluated differently. Different rules apply to them, even in how classroom space and computers can be shared with the rest of the school. Even the composition of a class matters, such as having minimum numbers of girls in particular classes. So it's useful to establish the context by explaining some of the history of CTE, the rules over CTE, and why canceling this particular class was such a big deal.

The Context

The history of CTE can be traced back to the early days of the United States. Schooling in America in the late eighteenth century, if any existed, often emphasized trade skills and was organized by trade unions or groups. Later, in the early 1800s, various "mechanical institutes" taught "mechanical arts" in cities across the country. These institutes included the Franklin Institute in Philadelphia (1824), the Maryland Institute for the Promotion of the Mechanic Arts in Baltimore (1826), and the Ohio Mechanics Institute in Cincinnati (1828).

Other schools that focused on manual labor opened throughout the nineteenth century. One school, Elmira College (1855), which was one of the first US women's colleges, required students to take courses in domestic sciences and general household affairs. By 1862 Congress had established the Land-Grant College Act, known as the Morrill Act, which provided states with land to create colleges specializing in agriculture and mechanical arts. Almost all of the resulting colleges were public, which hugely expanded access to higher education. The Morrill Act transformed engineering education in the US, and it made the country a leader in technical education.

Vocational education was formalized in 1917 by the Smith-Hughes National Vocational Education Act. This bill provided federal funds for vocational training in agriculture, trades and industry, and homemaking. It established the basic structure for organizing vocational education, as well as became the basis for the separation and isolation of vocational training from the rest of the curriculum in most schools. The act did this through two related mechanisms: one structural, the other financial.

The Smith-Hughes Act directed states to create plans for vocational education showing elements such as courses of study, equipment needed, and qualifications of teachers. Those plans had to be submitted by the state's board of education to the Federal Board for Vocational Education. However, federal law shaped these state plans, not state policy. This separation led many states to create separate boards of vocational education. Federal rules even mandated that students spend specific percentages of their school day in these classes—shop class (50 percent), related fields (25 percent), and academic coursework (25 percent), known as the 50-25-25 rule—which lasted until the 1960s.

The act also stipulated how vocational funds could be spent for both federal *and* state and local funding. For example, vocational funds could be spent on vocational teachers but not on regular academic teachers. While intended to preserve and maintain the viability of vocational education and prevent its funding from being "plundered" by other parts of the high school, the result was to create altogether separate operations. Combined with segregation of the curriculum as well as control over how students took courses, vocational education became an almost separate world that was disconnected from the rest of the high school.

From 1917 to now, vocational education has continued to grow. For example, in 1946, the George-Barden Act expanded vocational education beyond agriculture, trade, home economics, and industrial subjects. It added nursing and fishery occupations in 1956. In 1963 vocational funding became authorized by student populations rather than fields of study. Equal vocational opportunities were promoted for women and girls in 1976. Business partnerships and academic integration were embraced in 1990. And 1998 saw a conscious shift from job-specific training to skill-based career education.

In 2006 the federal legislation governing vocational education (known as the Perkins Acts—there's an original bill, plus four reauthorizations), officially replaced the term *vocational education* with *career and technical education*. Current annual federal investment in CTE stands at around $1.4 billion. Texas now has fourteen clustered programs of study that include many subfields from welding to graphic design to oil and gas exploration to lodging and resort management.

While CTE isn't as segregated from the rest of the high school as it used to be, divisions still exist. Some of this remaining segregation is mental in that many people still maintain perceptual silos around and between CTE and academic coursework, perhaps from its long historical division.[17] However, other separations are tangible. For example, unlike academic courses, which fall under the STAAR accountability system, CTE classes are assessed under accountability through the number of industry-based certifications (IBC) students earn and through the number of courses students take in a particular program of study.

In Texas for the 2022–2024 school years, students have been able to select from 293 different IBCs ranging from agricultural biotechnology to medical coding and billing. The state of Texas includes IBCs within its accountability rating system for schools. So besides any professional or occupational benefits students might receive from earning IBCs, IBCs are important to schools because of their connection to the accountability rating. This means, of course, that students need to be able to take the classes to earn the certifications—which can be a problem because finding qualified people to teach those classes is difficult.

Another difference involves funding. Schools in Texas are funded in part based on students' average daily attendance rate. Students might miss, say, the first hour of the day, or perhaps they'll leave school an hour early for an appointment. But as long as they are present when attendance is taken, they are counted present for the day. CTE counts attendance differently. Attendance is based on actual "contact" hours, hours that students actually spend in CTE classes.[18] Yet schools receive substantially more funding for attendance in CTE classes than in regular classes—between 10 percent and 47 percent more funding for the same amount of attendance.[19]

Compounding those pressures are shortage pressures. Just like other teaching areas, CTE faces a teacher shortage.[20] One reason for this shortage might be the difficulty in earning the certification to teach CTE classes. Not only do CTE teachers need the Texas teacher certification and to complete a Texas teacher preparation program, they also need a degree and/or licensure in the particular field, as well as real-world practice / work experience in that field. This shortage can force school districts to share CTE teachers across multiple campuses. Sometimes districts even bus students from one school to the next to take particular CTE courses.

The Problem

So canceling this class was complicated. Well, it was simple, according to school district policy. But in practice, the decision involved many moving parts, all of which exerted power: some students had to take the class, or they wouldn't complete their IBC on time; canceling the class meant lost funding for the district; the CTE teacher was likely already stretched from accommodating the district's CTE needs and now would be teaching one less section; and resources would go unused if that class didn't make it. Here's the story.

In Tomas's school district, if enrollment is too low in a class, principals are supposed to cancel the class and reassign students to other classes. Just before classes started one recent school year, Tomas checked the master schedule at his high school and found that one CTE class had too few students. He explained that "sometimes the program is just not that popular, so those are really tough decisions that you have to make, because it can mess up a pathway for kids to earn an IBC." So he cancelled the class. Tomas said that afterwards, he "didn't think anything of it."

But three weeks into the school year, he said, "I got a call from the assistant superintendent telling me that kids are saying, 'Hey, they don't care about our program.'" The assistant superintendent told Tomas to reinstate the class. But this was no small feat. Changing the master schedule at that late date is hard. There are moving pieces to coordinate, lost teaching time to make up, and numerous other teachers to inconvenience because of the changes. Tomas said, "You can imagine the problems this creates. We're three weeks into the school year. The master schedule is already set. But now you have to add these seven kids? It was just disastrous."

Tomas feels certain that students and parents—and possibly even the CTE teacher of the canceled class—pushed behind the scenes for the class to be reinstated. This makes sense. Why else would the assistant superintendent make this change except to appease complaining parents? Tomas explained, "I guarantee that there were parents involved with this decision. And I want to clarify that we did think about how this would impact kids. But down the line, you have to make a decision—seven kids enrolled? Kill it. And then, all of a sudden, this happens."

This happened in the beginning of Tomas's first year as principal. He learned from the experience. In his second and third years as principal, he no longer cancelled CTE classes if they had too low an enrollment. He didn't ask permission; he just did it. And then, when he eventually received a call from the same assistant superintendent asking why particular CTE classes were too small, Tomas thought (but didn't say), "Didn't we just go through this? It doesn't matter. The kids just have to complain, and you're going to tell me to reinstate the class. Why do this dance? Don't make me the bad guy. Let me be the good guy; I'm saving this class."

Story No. 3: Firing a Low-Performing Teacher

This last story illustrates the power embedded within a decision that Lionel, the elementary principal, had to make regarding whether or not to fire a low-performing teacher. At a glance, it seems like firing a low-performing teacher would be an easy call and well within Lionel's power. Students deserve good teachers, and a school's rating depends a lot on having quality teachers. If teachers can't raise students' learning and test scores to the level they need to be, then those teachers need to go so principals can find better teachers to teach those students. It turns out, however, that it's not quite that simple.

The Context

The saying goes "It's hard to find good help." This is especially true in a labor market in which schools struggle to hire and retain quality teachers and in which almost one-half, by some estimates, of new teachers leave teaching within their first five years.[21] The year-to-year attrition is also high. In Texas an average of 11 percent of teachers have left teaching across the state each year for the past five years (2018–2023 school years).[22] Further, in one 2021 poll, a startling high percentage (68 percent) of teachers reported considering leaving teaching the following year.[23]

So firing a low-performing teacher in this labor market is no small task. Hiring and firing decisions are, of course, crucial elements within any organization. But they're fraught with problems. For one, they're expensive. Estimates of the cost for organizations to hire new staff range from around $4,000 to almost $20,000, depending on the type of position. It can also take organizations up to forty-two days to fill a position. Further, some estimates suggest that it can take up to eight months for a new hire to achieve optimum productivity at the new job.[24]

Firing employees also comes with costs in addition to the costs of hiring someone to fill that vacated position. These costs are both direct and indirect. Overtime and severance might need to be paid. Companies, for example, often must pay the Consolidated Omnibus Budget Reconciliation Act (COBRA) health insurance premiums for former employees, perhaps for up to thirty-six months. Expensive temporary employees might be needed to cover the position. Existing employees might experience reduced productivity or overwork if that former employee's work is completed by existing staff. If lawsuits get filed, legal fees can easily run many more thousands of dollars.

In terms of schools, hiring decisions are also complicated by the difficulty in identifying effective teachers at the hiring stage.[25] Licensure requirements alone do not guarantee good teaching. One problem involves technical aspects of certification exams. For example, test items are easily susceptible to what's called *construct irrelevant variance*. This means that test items might require, say, good short-term memory (perhaps by including lots of initial explanation or other stimulus material), which is likely to be irrelevant to the content the test item purports to measure.[26]

Ideally, principals would schedule multiple demonstration lessons for job candidates to teach, observing each one and debriefing with the applicant afterwards. Even that idea, though, would not reveal a complete picture of an applicant's teaching effectiveness, since it would not show how applicants interact and build learning relationships with students over time. But even that plan is not viable, of course, which leaves principals stuck with using somewhat lacking licensure requirements, references, and their own imperfect interviewing skills to hire new teachers.

Additionally, school administrators must consider the impact firing decisions have on student achievement. Principals don't just manage processes for making better widgets (as if that in itself is easy, which it isn't); the "widgets" (i.e., students) that principals ultimately manage have their own feelings and opinions about the management process. Since students think for themselves, they might and frequently do react negatively to firing decisions. And when students react negatively to firing decisions, their achievement often drops.

Further, it's hard to forecast the effects of firing decisions because "identifying the net effects of teacher turnover is difficult."[27] For example, sometimes teachers leave not simply a campus but teaching altogether. In those cases, researchers just measure the before and after effects inside a school. In other cases, though, teachers leave one campus to go work at a different campus. The before and after achievement at both campuses would need to be measured and compared. Further, variables such as the proficiency of all the teachers involved, as well as that of when during the school year the teachers left or arrived at a school, should all be measured.

The overall picture from the research on teacher turnover, however, is complicated and even contradictory at times. First, it's important to recognize that teacher turnover usually hurts student achievement in low-performing schools more than it does in high-performing schools. For instance, one study, which estimated the effects of turnover on over six hundred thousand New York City fourth- and fifth-grade students over five years, found that the harmful effects on ELA achievement were generally two to four times stronger in schools with lower-performing students than schools with generally higher-performing students.[28]

This study also found that teacher turnover reduces the achievement of students in the neighboring class, with teachers who stayed in the same school and grade level. The researchers suggest "that the rotation of teachers has an influence beyond just those students of teachers who stayed in the same school from year to year."[29] Indeed, they hold that "there is a consistent pattern for stayers—in lower achieving schools, their students perform significantly worse when turnover is greater.[30]

A study in a large school district in Texas supported those findings. This study found that teachers "exiting from Texas schools are roughly 50 percent of a teacher standard deviation less effective than their colleagues who remain on the same campus."[31] Further, the study found that even teachers who switch campuses within the same district are less effective than teachers who stay on a campus. The study concluded by declaring that "[the] net turnover adversely affects the quality of instruction in lower-achievement schools . . . due to loss of general and grade-specific experience that is sufficient to offset potential gains from the departed teachers."[32]

Yet a different study contrasted these typical findings about the negative effects of teacher turnover. This study took place in District of Columbia Public Schools (DCPS) and lasted three years across the entire district. The study measured the effect of a new teacher evaluation and retention system implemented by DCPS that used a performance assessment system to manage teacher effectiveness.[33]

In short, teachers with multiple low ratings were exited from DCPS, and teachers with high ratings were financially rewarded to stay in their positions at their schools. The exited teachers were replaced by teachers the district found to be more effective. The study observed that student achievement grew by 21 percent of a standard deviation in math and 14 percent of a standard deviation in reading when low-performing teachers were replaced by more effective teachers. This finding suggests that teacher turnover might produce positive effects if both low-performing teachers and high-performing replacements can be identified.

The time of year that teachers leave and are replaced can also play an important role in student achievement. Unsurprisingly, research finds that teacher turnover during the school year hurts student achievement more than during the summer between school years. Students' learning gets disrupted as they experience various short- and long-term substitutes until a new teacher is hired, as they have to adjust to new teaching practices and personalities, and as they try to create new relationships with those newly hired personnel.[34]

One study found that when students lose a teacher during the school year (and another teacher is hired as a replacement), their test score gains are approximately 7.5 percent of a standard deviation lower than students who did not lose a teacher.[35] A different study found that hiring teachers after the school year starts reduced student achievement in math by 4.2 percent of a standard deviation and by 2.6 percent of a standard deviation in comparison with students of new teachers who were hired during the summer before school starts. These differences are large, equaling weeks to months of lost instructional gains.[36]

The authors of this second study have traced a number of *disruption effects* likely related to those learning losses. For example, the best new teachers available that year have likely already been hired before school started, and replacement teachers are also likely to be either new or not that experienced. Late hires have less time to establish productive norms and relationships with students, and they must realign classes that have already experienced one or more teachers that year. Further, the teachers have less time to develop new learning activities and lesson plans, as well as to learn new practices, policies, and procedures for the new school.

Last, teacher turnover can destabilize the teaching staff at a school. This is especially possible when teachers are let go due to high-stakes teacher evaluations. One study noted that if teachers perceive no significant differences between themselves and the terminated teachers, they may feel at equal risk of being fired.[37] This teacher stress can lead to lower self-efficacy, worse teacher-student rapport, and lower teacher effectiveness.[38] To be clear, this isn't to state that these effects *will* result from teacher turnover, only that they *may* happen as policies are instituted to fire teachers due to low high-stakes test scores.

The Problem

It was in this fraught environment, one with no clearly best answers, that Lionel had to decide whether or not to fire a low-performing teacher. He knew he had the power and authority to make the move. He knew that students deserved better and that central administration would likely not contest firing the teacher. But Lionel was also able to recognize that the web of power produced unintended consequences, so he knew he had to act cautiously.

The story itself is simple. A teacher in Lionel's school was struggling. The teacher taught in a STAAR-tested grade level, and her scores were always low—"really bad," as Lionel put it.[39] Combine this with the fact that Lionel was working to turn around his school. He had only been principal at his elementary school for a short while. When he started as principal, the school had perhaps the lowest test scores in the school district, so waiting and hoping that the teacher would quickly improve wasn't an enticing option; Lionel needed to make changes soon.

In addition to the research showing that firing that teacher would bring uncertain results, especially depending on the time of year when the teacher would be fired and a replacement hired, Lionel was aware of another complication: the teacher was well liked and supported by the other teachers on her grade level. Lionel framed the problem like this: "The other two grade teachers are carrying a lot of her weight. They're helping her plan. So I know if I try to get rid of this teacher, I'll lose two good teachers too. So I go in there and be supportive, but that person is connected to two other amazing teachers that make our school great, so you gotta be careful there too."

Lionel sensed the possible consequences of firing the teacher. He even framed the situation in terms of power, having stated, "So in a sense she has the power, because I can't really get rid of her because I'm going to mess up the entire culture of that grade level." So Lionel decided not to fire the teacher. Instead, he changed the way that he supervised both the teacher and the grade level. For example, he switched his meetings with them from directive to collaborative.

He still meets with the team every other week, but instead of meeting with them in his office, the "principal's office," which can be intimidating, he goes to them, to their classrooms, while they plan together as a team. He no longer leads the meetings. Now he listens as the team plans and joins the conversations as necessary, trying to guide them in their planning: "Try this or that resource," or "Be sure to incorporate this element into your lesson"—those kinds of input. Is he surveilling them? Of course. But it's done in a more cooperative and nonthreatening manner as he tries to help steer their thoughts about teaching toward his goals for the school.

In a way, this example is a sort of "non-example" in that nothing happened, no unintended consequences caused any problems. Bad things were avoided, and the school kept improving. But that's because Lionel was able to forecast those potential bad results and avoid them. The web of power was still there; Lionel just didn't get caught in it that time. For *that* to happen, however, big changes had to occur.

So lots of things actually happened. Lionel set aside his own power to bolster the power of the grade-level team. He changed how, where, and why he supervised the teachers, allowing and encouraging their strengths to blossom. Lionel was able to *not* pull on the web of power and instead submit, in a way, to the wishes and strengths of his team, not resisting *their* pulling on the web. As he put it, "I have to give and take."

WHAT'S THE TAKEAWAY?

The examples of power examined throughout this book are hard to see in practice. Unless they're vocalized, one can't see students' beliefs (chapter 3). Teachers don't usually advertise their decision-making processes (chapter 4). And while teachers experience initiatives, it's difficult to see the initiatives' combined impact on teachers (chapter 5). This chapter continues this pattern by examining even more hidden iterations of power. Lionel was able to guess the potential effects of power, but he couldn't see it in action. Tomas only saw the effects of power *after* they occurred. And Hector could only see the effects of power at a distance as he visited different schools.

All three of these stories vividly illustrate how power works as a web: you make a decision over here, and an (often unanticipated) effect from that decision pops up somewhere else, like pulling on a web. The nature of the web makes it hard to see power working behind the scenes. Tomas, for example, couldn't have guessed that students, parents, and maybe even the CTE teacher would exert power behind the scenes onto the assistant superintendent and successfully pressure her to reinstate the course. Tomas was a new principal and hadn't experienced that situation before. For all he knew, people would follow the district's rules.

Until he saw it, Hector wouldn't have guessed that elementary school principals in his district would alter the testing procedures—and, as a result, the teaching practices—for dual-language students, based, Hector thought, on what seemed best for a particular school, not on what was best for students' dual-language goals. Nor could he know the actual extent of the problem, except that it was more than a few schools. The school district advertises that program, so it seemed logical to assume that administrators would manage it with fidelity.

Lionel was able to predict a potential ramification with firing that low-performing teacher. But he held an advantage over Tomas and Hector: he knew who the players were. He knew who might exert power if he fired the teacher; they were right in front of him. He knew the teachers' temperaments. He knew the relationships within that team. He knew that the other teachers were trying to help that struggling teacher. So it wasn't hard for him to guess that if he fired the weaker teacher, he might end up losing all three teachers.

Tomas and Hector knew none of this information, which illustrates the difficulty of operating within the web of power. It's not as if they could avoid the web, though. Nobody working in schools can. The web exists because people have choices about when they act, and those actions always influence *other* people's actions. Further, just because power can operate out of sight, doesn't make it any less effective. These, then, are perhaps the two most obvious takeaways from these stories: you can't always easily determine who is working behind the scenes within the web of power, and it's hard to predict the consequences of your actions.

It's useful to consider how these experiences impacted these three educators. Both Tomas and Lionel experienced the contingent nature of their power as principals. Neither could make an executive decision in these cases and suffer no ramifications. Tomas was explicitly told to reverse his decision. While Lionel never received such a command, he recognized the even worse consequences he might face if he fired that low-performing teacher. Hector also faced frustration at his own contingent power: he could advocate for dual-language practices but was overruled repeatedly in the name of accountability to ratings over dual-language fidelity.

As a result, Tomas and Hector grew more cynical about operating decisions. They saw how decisions about district policies functioned more like a game than as fidelity to meaningful practices. They saw how policies were fluid, more akin to easily revised points of reference than to reliable standards. Hector learned that his dual-language program was important to the district but only conditionally important relative to test scores. Tomas learned to ignore district policy on minimum CTE class sizes and to keep small classes open, lest he repeat that drama.

Lionel didn't grow cynical, but he certainly grew more cautious. He clearly expressed the limits of his power by stating, "[The teacher] has the power, because I can't really get rid of her, because I'm going to mess up the entire culture of the grade level." Was Lionel's belief correct? He'll never know. In practice it matters little, since there's no denying the constraint Lionel felt. Will he always be restricted from firing staff? Of course not. Power dynamics across the web change and vary by situation. In this case, the teacher was low performing but not so low that she had to go regardless of consequences. And the team was strong; next time, it may not be.

All decisions produce consequences. What makes working within the web of power so tricky is the combination of often not knowing who else is exerting power, where or how that power will manifest, and what consequences might result. It's not exactly like working in the dark, but it's close. As Lionel's story shows, sometimes the web presents itself clearly. But usually the web works like it did in Hector's and Tomas's stories: it is obscure and hard to see. That doesn't mean, however, that people are helpless.

Take the stories of school initiatives from chapter 5. Initiatives also pull on the web. Administrators have a duty to try to forecast how their initiatives (and other actions) interact with other forces in the web, such as other initiatives, technology requirements, testing demands, and more. Principals and superintendents might not always guess the consequences correctly. But the effort is crucial if they want to better run schools because, sometimes, they'll get it right.

NOTES

1. Henri Bergson, *Creative evolution* (New York: Philosophical Library, 1946), 28.
2. William H. Ittelson and Hadley Cantril, *Perception: A transactional approach* (New York: Doubleday & Co., 1954), 29.
3. This observation has been repeatedly reaffirmed by research at least since 1925. For example, see Frederick H. Lund, "The psychology of belief," *Journal of Abnormal and Social Psychology* 20 (1925): 23; and Samuel P. Hayes, "The predictive ability of voters," *Journal of Social Psychology* 7 (1936): 183.
4. J. Richard Eiser and Christine Eiser, "Prediction of environmental change: Wish-fulfillment revisited," *European Journal of Social Psychology* 5, no. 3 (1975): 315.
5. Moshe Bar, ed., *Predictions in the brain: Using our past to generate a future* (New York: Oxford University Press, 2011).
6. Caroline Beaton, "Humans are bad at predicting futures that don't benefit them," *The Atlantic*, November, 2, 2017, https://www.theatlantic.com/science/archive/2017/11/humans-are-bad-at-predicting-futures-that-dont-benefit-them/544709/
7. Beaton, "Humans are bad at predicting futures."
8. Raymond S. Nickerson, "Confirmation bias: A ubiquitous phenomenon in many guises," *Review of General Psychology* 2, no. 2 (June 1998): 175.
9. Neil D. Weinstein, "Unrealistic optimism about future life events," *Journal of Personality and Social Psychology* 39, no. 5 (November 1980): 806.
10. Ambrose Bierce, *The devil's dictionary* (New York: World Publishing Company, 1911), 12.
11. Foucault, *The history of sexuality*, 96.
12. Foucault, *Power*, 343.
13. These are not listed in order. To help maintain the participants' anonymity, no identifying details are presented, nor should they be inferred.
14. Foucault, *Power*, 345.
15. These are the standard testing practices. Allowances can be made depending on factors such as if the student is new to a school district or has no understanding of English.
16. Reading and math are tested in grades 3–5. Science is tested in grade 5. There is no test for social studies at the elementary level, but if that were to change, it would likely be tested also in Spanish.
17. Donna Pearson, "CTE and the Common Core can address the problem of silos," *Phi Delta Kappan* 96, no. 6 (February 2015): 12.
18. Texas Education Agency, "Funding for CTE," accessed on May 24, 2023, https://tea.texas.gov/finance-and https://texasgateway.org/resource/lesson-4-cte-funding-and-attendance-accounting?binder_id=124791.

19. Texas Education Agency, "Career and Technology Funding Allotment," accessed on May 24, 2023, https://tea.texas.gov/finance-and-grants/state-funding/additional-finance-resources/career-and-technology-education-allotment.

20. See media statement from Ryan Franklin, associate commissioner of educator leadership and quality, January 30, 2020, https://tea.texas.gov/about-tea/news-and-multimedia/correspondence/taa-letters/2020-2021-teacher-shortage-areas-and-loan-forgiveness-programs.

21. Emma Garcia and Elaine Weiss, *Examining the factors that play a role in the teacher shortage crisis: Key findings from EPI's 'Perfect Storm in the Teacher Labor Market' series* (Washington, DC: Economic Policy Institute, 2020), https://files.eric.ed.gov/fulltext/ED611183.pdf.; Texas Education Agency, "Teacher retention by preparation route 2011–12 through 2021–22," published March 2023, https://tea.texas.gov/sites/default/files/teacher-retention-by-preparation-route.pdf.

22. Texas Education Agency, "Employed teacher attrition and new hires 2011–12 through 2022–23," published March 2023, https://tea.texas.gov/reports-and-data/educator-data/employed-teacher-attrition-and-new-hires.pdf.

23. Brian Lopez, "It's not just Covid-19: Why Texas faces a teacher shortage," *The Texas Tribune*, July 25, 2022, https://www.texastribune.org/2022/07/25/texas-teacher-shortage/.

24. These costs include expenses such as job sourcing, background checks, drug testing, prehire assessments, recruitment outsourcing, marketing, referral rewards, and more. Costs will increase as the skills and experience required for the position increase. For more information see the following blogs: Elsie Boskamp, "25+ crucial average costs per hire facts [2023]: All cost of hiring statistics," *Zippia*, February 16, 2023, https://www.zippia.com/advice/cost-of-hiring-statistics-average-cost-per-hire/; and Glassdoor Team, "How to calculate cost-per-hire," *Glassdoor for Employers*, July 5, 2019, https://www.glassdoor.com/employers/blog/calculate-cost-per-hire/.

25. Jonah E. Rockoff and Cecilia Speroni, "Subjective and objective evaluations of teacher effectiveness," *The American Economic Review* 100, no. 2 (May 2010): 261.

26. David C. Berliner, "The near impossibility of testing for teacher quality," *Journal of Teacher Education* 56, no. 3 (2005): 205.

27. Eric A. Hanushek, Steven G. Rivkin, and Jeffrey C. Schiman, "Dynamic effects of teacher turnover on the quality of instruction," *Economics of education Review* 55, (2016): 132.

28. Matthew Ronfeldt et al., "How teacher turnover harms student achievement," National Bureau of Economic Research, Working Paper 17176, June 2011, http://www.nber.org/papers/w17176.

29. Ronfeldt et al., "How teacher turnover harms student achievement," 16.

30. Ronfeldt et al., "How teacher turnover harms student achievement," 16.

31. Hanushek, Rivkin, and Schiman, "Dynamic effects of teacher turnover," 137.

32. Hanushek, Rivkin, and Schiman, "Dynamic effects of teacher turnover," 145.

33. Melissa Adnot et al., "Teacher turnover, teacher quality, and student achievement in DCPS," National Bureau of Economic Research, Working Paper 21922, January 2016, http://www.nber.org/papers/w21922.

34. Gary T. Henry and Christopher Redding, "The consequences of leaving school early: The effects of within-year and end-of-year teacher turnover," *Education Finance & Policy* 15, no. 2 (2018): 332.

35. Henry and Redding, "The consequences of leaving school early," 332.

36. John J. Papay and Matthew A. Kraft, "The productivity costs of inefficient hiring practices: Evidence from late teacher hiring," *Journal of Policy Analysis and Management* 35, no. 4 (June 2016): 791.

37. Robert Folger and Mary A. Konovsky, "Effects of procedural and distributive justice on reactions to pay raise decisions," *Academy of Management Journal* 32, no. 1 (March 1989): 115.

38. For teacher self-efficacy, see Fernando D. Betoret, "Stressors, self-efficacy, coping resources, and burnout among secondary school teachers in Spain," *Educational Psychology* 26 (2006): 519. For teacher-student rapport and teaching effectiveness, see Millicent H. Abel and Joanne Sewell, "Stress and burnout in rural and urban secondary school teachers," *The Journal of Educational Research* 92, no. 5 (1999): 287.

39. STAAR is the acronym for the state accountability system in Texas (State of Texas Assessments of Academic Readiness). In elementary schools, students take STAAR exams in third, fourth, and fifth grades. To help maintain the privacy of the teacher, the specific grade level won't be stated. This doesn't change the analysis or impact; school officials want STAAR scores to be high in all grade levels.

Chapter 7

Why the "Big Stuff" Isn't the Biggest

The previous four chapters pointed a detailed, high-resolution light on specific examples of power in schools. This is the "small stuff," the everyday examples of power that people routinely and repeatedly negotiate in schools. But perhaps you're still not convinced that the small stuff is just as powerful—and likely even more powerful—than the "big stuff" you hear about on the news. Perhaps you still feel that the big stuff has to be a more powerful influence on schools—or people wouldn't focus on it so much.

This point is crucial. If the big stuff exerts more influence on schools than the small stuff, then the analysis in the preceding chapters is flawed. That would mean that this book is just plain wrong. The big stuff follows action/reaction thinking about power: this would mean that the reform effort or the political mandate or the standardized test (or whatever other big thing) essentially gives directions to schools and teachers, which schools and teachers follow. So if it really is the biggest influence, then power in schools would primarily follow an action/reaction model instead of the web model that is advocated for here.

But the big stuff doesn't exert the most influence, even though it seems like it does. Big public factors are easy to see and seem easy to understand. Maybe that's part of the reason why people are so drawn to them and attribute so much power to them. After all, it's hard to analyze what you can't really see, and the examples in chapters 3 to 6 are mostly hidden from public view and never receive the publicity of the big stuff.

This chapter takes two well-known examples of big, public influences on schools—high-stakes accountability testing and school reform—and, using evidence from chapters 3 to 6, illustrates why those factors do not exert more power on schools than the small stuff. Some sources might lead you to believe that these examples produce unmitigated changes, as if teachers and schools merely react to the dictates and demands of high-stakes testing and reform efforts. But those changes are actually always mediated by teachers and schools, which means that they're not as powerful as people make them out to be.

THE LIMITED POWER OF HIGH-STAKES TESTING

You might think that standardized testing, particularly high-stakes accountability testing for public school students (known in Texas as STAAR), impacts schooling more than other factors. High-stakes testing certainly seems to fall under a Machiavellian way of thinking about power: tests *make* teachers teach to them, tests *make* schools do lots of test preps, and tests *make* schools align their curriculum to the content of the test. Or so the thinking goes. Perhaps you've seen other evidence, too, such as STAAR parades in elementary schools,[1] school ratings driven by test scores, and real estate values connected to test scores.[2]

Studies in this vein contend that high-stakes testing acts as a form of labor control over teachers' work,[3] limiting opportunities for inquiry and "student-centered" learning while emphasizing more "teacher-centered" strategies.[4] Indeed, many researchers claim that not only does high-stakes testing exert a deleterious impact on how teachers teach, but it is also the primary influence on their teaching.[5] Empirical evidence supports these assertions.

For instance, a study in Kentucky finds that middle school teachers "felt strongly that the [high-stakes] assessment weighed heavily on their minds" and that they "resorted to 'coverage' over in-depth study of instructional topics."[6] A different study argues that testing fosters a "just the facts, ma'am" approach to teaching.[7] Yet another study claims that "because multiple-choice testing leads to multiple-choice teaching, the methods that teachers have in their arsenal become reduced, and teaching work is deskilled."[8]

However, this is not the whole story. Many other researchers present evidence of teachers teaching in meaningful and productive ways *despite* high-stakes testing. For example, teachers *can* find ways to create constructivist classrooms within high-stakes testing environments.[9] Teachers *can* generate "thoughtfulness" within their students inside these classrooms.[10] Additionally, this author has documented Margaret, Bill, and Mary (the three teachers whose work was examined in chapter 4) engaging students in meaningful, inquiry-based learning, even within the pressure of both high-stakes testing and AYP.[11]

Why is there the discrepancy? Why do some researchers insist that high-stakes testing restricts teachers' ability to do meaningful teaching (and present evidence to that effect), but other researchers present evidence that makes the opposite case? Why do some teachers see testing as an insurmountable obstacle, but others find ways to work around it? Is one side lying or fabricating evidence? No. The evidence exists to support both cases; both cases are made sincerely.

The answer has to do with the mindset, the thinking, and the beliefs of teachers and researchers—which includes how they think about power in schools. Some teachers and researchers just seem to think about power more like Machiavelli than like Foucault, and that thinking limits the teaching possibilities they can imagine. Indeed, many researchers argue that teachers' knowledge and beliefs about teaching and about their content exert a greater influence on their teaching than does high-stakes testing.[12]

The researchers and teachers who think more like Foucault understand that teachers *always* have power to adjust their teaching to new challenges, even when those challenges seem formidable. This doesn't mean that testing never gets in the way. It does. For example, as discussed in chapter 4, Margaret once lamented that she had to cut out an activity on Washington crossing the Delaware, a popular dramatic activity in which her students used butcher paper to make a large boat and then reenacted the iconic painting by Emanuel Leutze.

Her decision resulted from pacing concerns regarding district benchmark exams. But she retained another dramatic activity on the English Civil War in which she dressed up as a queen (representing the British monarchy) and, as she explained the events of that war, used a large blow-up balloon axe to "chop off" students' heads. So while testing presented obstacles and did cause her to remove an activity she enjoyed, she found a way to still do things with her students that she wanted to do.

Two other examples from chapter 4 also help illustrate why high-stakes testing does not impose power on teachers in a Machiavellian sense. The first involves content. Teachers must teach content that is on a test. High-stakes testing is often criticized for forcing teachers to "teach to the test." But this criticism misunderstands that teachers should *always* teach to a test. That is, teachers always have to prepare students for however they will be assessed.

A popular lesson design practice called *backwards design* is based on this premise. You identify the objectives, you design the assessments, and then you plan the instruction—in that order. That way, teachers know in advance how students will be assessed, and they can ensure that they prepare students as best they can for those assessments. To put it differently, would it be good teaching if teachers *didn't* prepare students for their assessments, or if they *didn't* help students be successful? Of course not. That would be negligent.

The question, then, is not about teaching to a test. The question is about what content will get taught. Texas, like other states, has a state curriculum. Local school districts don't determine the content that kids will learn. The state does. In Texas, this is known as the Texas Essential Knowledge and

Skills (TEKS). The STAAR is based on the TEKS. Now, a common and valid criticism of the STAAR is that it tests too much content, leading to what Bill Trammell (as well as many other teachers) have called a "mile wide and inch deep" approach to teaching.

Teachers struggle with this everywhere, not just in Texas. It's too much content, which makes it difficult for teachers to get through it by the end of the school year—hence the common focus on coverage. Yet, contrary to popular belief, this is not a problem created by high-stakes testing. The tests just assess the state curriculum. Take something out of that curriculum, out of that long list of content in every area, and—voila!—there's much less content to cover.

But get this—teachers can feel reluctant to delete content! Margaret is a great example. As discussed in chapter 4, if given the opportunity, she would delete almost none of the TEKS for her subject, eighth-grade US history. She explained her thinking as follows: "Overall, you're asking a history teacher to leave out part of history. One thing connects to another. What are you going to leave out?" Thus, high-stakes testing doesn't impose a content or a coverage burden onto teachers. The state curriculum does that. And if teachers could, they might not want to delete any of that content, meaning the coverage problem is, in some ways, self-reinforced.

The second example involves scope and sequence. School districts organize content for all classes, providing structure to the TEKS. The TEKS simply lists content to be studied during a school year; it doesn't specify in what order or how long that content should be studied. Because it would likely create a mess if individual classroom teachers had to determine the scope and sequence for their own classes, school districts sequence that content for them and indicate how many days or weeks teachers should spend on it.

Early in the study, Margaret, Bill, Mary, and Orlando's school district used a curriculum management system called CSCOPE (which has since been renamed the TEKS Resource System). CSCOPE was created by Texas education service centers, and it was used by over eight hundred school districts, charter schools, and private schools. CSCOPE created tight pacing demands to cover their social studies content, and it was enforced through district-wide benchmark exams. According to Bill, "with CSCOPE, you have an outline you can build from, but you're expected to hit certain marks by certain times."

The timeline and pacing demands created by CSCOPE and other curriculum management systems can feel burdensome to teachers. But even with that burden, teachers can still exert power. In chapter 4, you saw Mary revise the district scope and sequence for a part of her sixth-grade social studies class, the part on Central and South America. Mary didn't ask permission. She didn't even tell her administration that she had made the change. She just did it. Based on her expertise and experience teaching that course, she knew the change would work more effectively with her students.

So Mary and Margaret still had power. Neither CSCOPE nor the coverage pressures took away their power. Mary had to use her power wisely because she might have faced repercussions if it hadn't worked. And Margaret, even with feeling burdened by the "testing apparatus,"[13] wouldn't delete content if given the chance. Also notice that Mary didn't want to delete any content. She just wanted to change the way she taught that content.

THE LIMITED POWER OF SCHOOL REFORM

The research on school reform teaches three main points:

1. School reform efforts aren't monolithic. Just because people hear about them a lot doesn't mean that they always produce big changes.
2. The type of change suggested matters. In short, the further a reform is from typical practice, the less likely it will succeed. And,
3. Schools change reforms. Reforms are never implemented as is, as though they were cut and pasted into the school. No, schools always adapt, revise, and sometimes even slowly strangle reforms.

The label "school reform" refers to efforts to change the way schools operate. These efforts can come from anywhere: government agencies, nonprofit organizations, foundations, political parties, and more. Reforms have focused on everything from teaching to administration to the physical design of schools. School reform efforts have existed as long as there have been schools: because schools are social and political creations, people have always tried to make and remake schools for different purposes.

Reformers' goals have changed over the years. In the mid-1800s, the graded school was a big reform that changed the structure of schooling from the one-room schoolhouse to schools divided into age-correlated grades. In the early twentieth century, the Carnegie unit began to divide courses into credits that could be tallied and accounted for. Segregation was the big reform in the years after 1954. Later in the twentieth century, reformers focused on goals like school accountability and a more demanding curriculum. Today, goals for some reformers might include social and emotional learning, as well as diversity, inclusion, and equity.

People often think that these kinds of big-change efforts make big impacts on schools. After all, when they're current and popular, you hear about them everywhere: politicians, columnists, education leaders, industry leaders, and others will talk about them, sometimes ad nauseum, proclaiming how important the changes will be—until the reform efforts fail. And they often do. Remember "new math" from the 1960s, the open classrooms from the 1970s, the community-run schools, and the nongraded schools? Lately, some might add Common Core standards to that list of failed reforms (even though it's likely too early to tell in that case).

Not all reforms fail, though, and not all failed reforms remain failed. Take school vouchers. They failed in the 1980s. But as of 2021, "more than 600,000 students [across thirty-two states] participated in a voucher, scholarship tax credit, or education savings account program."[14] This means that as social, political, or economic conditions change, the potential for reforms to "stick" changes too. There are reasons for this, and those reasons—even the fact that a failed reform is not necessarily a failed reform in the future—offer evidence that reform efforts aren't the monolith people think they are. Indeed, while they can be "big," they often aren't.

Why, then, do some reforms succeed while others fail? The answer requires context. The fundamental structures of schooling that exist today were established long ago: high school courses taken for credits, schools organized by age-specific grades, more or less standardized subjects like biology and geography, teachers who usually teach alone in classrooms, and more. Education scholars David Tyack and William Tobin label these structures the "grammar of schooling"; by "grammar of schooling," they refer to "the regular structures and rules that organize the work of instruction."[15]

This grammar of schooling has become so ingrained in the psyche of the American public, in their understanding of what a school is, that it "has become taken for granted as just the way schools are. It is the *departure* from customary school practice that attracts attention."[16] Consider this claim for yourself. Should a single elementary school classroom have 120 students and six teachers in it? Could they teach math that way in, say, the gym? Or would that be unusual? What about routinely enrolling eleven-year-olds in high school? Unusual too? But why? Schools are artificial creations, so can't they take whatever shape people want them to take?

The answer is no, because the public wouldn't let them. Take two early innovations in schooling: the graded school and the Carnegie unit. The first graded school, the Quincy Grammar School in Boston, opened in 1848. Over the next half century, graded schools quickly replaced one-room schoolhouses. The Carnegie unit was introduced in 1906, and by 1910, most secondary schools in the country used them.[17]

Both innovations were school reforms, but both succeeded. They were advanced by well-known and/or powerful people (Horace Mann for graded schools; Harvard University and other elite colleges for Carnegie units), and they were introduced at auspicious times in the development of schools. Now, though, they seem inevitable, as if they're a required component of schooling instead of just two early reforms that succeeded. They would be almost impossible to change for that reason—because they seem intrinsically part of schools. But they only feel that way because they are now a fundamental part of public thinking about what "real school" is.[18]

The scholar William Reid would probably have put this into an *institutional category* instead of an *organizational category*. Reid's division of schooling practices helps to further explain the hold that the grammar of schooling has on the American mind. The organizational category refers to curriculum delivery. What's more important here is the institutional category, which describes how entities and ideas "enter into the consciousness of the community at large."[19] Here, Reid helps describe how the notion of a "B student" holds popular significance unrelated to the specifics of any one student's specific experience.

So some kinds of changes are hard to push through. Other kinds of changes, though, happen all the time inside schools. Teachers change their teaching practices while schools change the amount of instructional time spent on different subjects, the courses they offer, how they teach reading, recess policies, policies for how students check out library books, and much, much more. Why do changes like these pass by usually unnoticed, but other changes completely fail? It seems like a paradox: schools have remained largely the same over the years, yet they also change all the time.

The answer has to do with public buy in and what kind of change is sought. It requires no additional public support for a teacher to change how she teaches, even if that change is fundamental and might hugely impact her students' learning. Indeed, almost nobody will know about it. Not the parents of her students (unless she tells them) and maybe not even her principal. But what if you try to change grading systems from letter or numerical grades to purely qualitative feedback? That would *definitely* require public support—which the school probably wouldn't get, at least not at first, because the change goes against common perceptions of real school.

The education scholar Larry Cuban describes this distinction as between "first-order" and "second-order" changes.[20] First-order changes build on what is familiar, on publicly accepted notions of schooling. Second-order changes seek to alter what is familiar. First-order changes typically require no public buy in, because they don't upset public perceptions of what schooling is. Put differently, first-order changes kind of already have public support since they don't upset the apple cart.[21] But second-order changes will require public support because somebody will notice how much they alter the typical way that schools operate.

It's crucial to remember, however, that even if a reform makes it into a school, the school will change the reform. Always. This usually happens in one of two ways: (1) reforms get assimilated into existing school practices, or (2) school staff reject or modify how the reforms are implemented. For reforms to be successful, they must stay close to the teacher and "adapt their program to the daily needs and problems of classroom teachers."[22] Indeed, reform efforts "must take account of what teachers are ready to teach or ready to learn to teach."[23]

Reformers, especially critical reformers, routinely seem to forget the fact that teachers develop their practices over time, and they test reforms against what they know already works in their classrooms. This means that when teachers try a new curriculum model (or some other reform) and decide it doesn't work, "what they probably mean is that they could not find a way to address all of their concerns within the framework of that model."[24]

Two examples of early reforms that were changed by schools are kindergarten and junior high school. Kindergarten and junior high were initially created to meet the needs of specific kids. Kindergarten was intended to foster in young kids "social and intellectual development through organized games, music, gardening, art work, socialized play, and gymnastics."[25] Junior highs were carved out as special places for adolescents. They were created to prevent students from dropping out (when the post-fifth-grade dropout rate was high) by offering them vocational opportunities as well as challenging academically capable students.

Kindergarten and junior high schools succeeded, of course, but not in the format that reformers originally intended. Both were assimilated into existing structures. First-grade teachers had mixed feelings about the abilities of their new students, and school boards wanted to systematize the primary grades. Junior highs became patterned after high schools in part because of their ambiguous goals but also from the concern that the public perceive junior high schools as legitimate institutions.[26]

WHAT'S THE TAKE-AWAY?

Remember two thoughts when you finish this chapter: (1) even the factors that seem the most powerful are still mediated by public opinion and by the everyday actions of teachers and school staff, and (2) even though an influence might seem small and hard to see, it can still exert power. The big stuff can pull hard on the web of power. Lots of people talk and worry about the new state laws or the new testing guidelines or the new federal call to action. At times the big stuff can even appear to cancel the small stuff out completely. But that's an illusion—not the exertion of power by the big stuff but the notion that the big stuff swallows up the smaller stuff.

This is because the other influences on the web of power also tug at it. They're just harder to see, which is probably why they're so often missed.

Take the example from chapter 3. The definitions of giftedness stated by researchers and school leaders are public. They might be in the news. They certainly guide school policy. So they're easy to see. But as chapter 3 shows, students can hold complicated thoughts about giftedness that are hard to discover.

Nor is it easy to see how teachers revise school district curriculum plans, since they do it in their classrooms, usually unannounced, as you've seen in chapter 4. Or take the impact of initiatives from chapter 5 and the behind-the-scenes power from chapter 6. Teachers, principals, and instructional specialists certainly see and feel their immediate effects. But they're not public, so they don't garner public attention. They're still powerful, though.

NOTES

1. This is in Texas, of course. Other states might have parades with other names, such as a SOL parade in Virginia or an M-STEP parade in Michigan.

2. A 2017 *New York Times* article reports that "economists have estimated that within suburban neighborhoods, a 5% improvement in test scores can raise [home] prices by 2.5%." See Quoctrung Bui and Conor Dougherty, "Good schools, affordable homes: Finding the suburban sweet spots," *New York Times*, March 30, 2017, https://www.nytimes.com/interactive /2017/03/30/upshot/good-schools-affordable-homes-suburban-sweet-spots.html. Also, a Brookings Institute report states that "across the 100 largest metropolitan areas, housing costs an average of 2.4 times as much, or nearly $11,000 more per year, near a high-performing school tha[n] near a low-scoring public school." See Jonathan Rothwell, "Housing costs, zoning, and access to high-scoring schools," Brookings Institution, published April 19, 2012, https://www.brookings.edu/research/housing-costs-zoning-and-access-to-high-scoring-schools/.

3. Au, "Teaching under the new Taylorism," 25.

4. Wills, "Putting the squeeze on social studies," 1980; and Wills and Sandholtz, "Constrained professionalism," 1065.

5. Barksdale and Thomas, "What's at stake in high-stakes testing?" 384; Linda McNeil, *Contradictions of school reform: Educational costs of standardized testing* (New York: Routledge, 2000); Smith, "Put to the test," 8; and Kenneth E. Vogler, "The impact of high-stakes, state-mandated student performance assessment on teachers' instructional practices," *Education* 123, no. 1 (September 2002): 39.

6. Faulkner and Cook, "Testing vs. teaching," 7–8.

7. Vogler and Virtue, "'Just the facts, ma'am,'" 54.

8. Smith, "Put to the test," 10.

9. Williamson et al., "Meeting the challenge of high-stakes testing while remaining child-centered," 190.

10. Newmann, "Higher order thinking in teaching social studies," 41.

11. Jacob W. Neumann, "Examining mandated testing, teachers' milieu, *and* teachers' knowledge and beliefs: Gaining a fuller understanding of the web of influence on teachers' classroom practices," *Teachers College Record* 118, no. 2 (February 2016): 1.

12. Sandra Cimbricz, "State-mandated testing and teachers' beliefs and practices," *Education Policy Analysis Archives* 10, no. 2 (2002), http://epaa.asu.edu/epaa.v10n2.html; William A. Firestone et al., "The ambiguity of test preparation: A multimethod analysis in one state," *Teachers College Record* 104, no. 7 (October 2002): 1485–523; S. G. Grant, "An uncertain lever: Exploring the influence of state-level testing in New York State on teaching social studies," *Teachers College Record* 103, no. 3 (April 2001): 398–426; S. G. Grant, *History lessons: Teaching, learning, and testing in United States high school classrooms* (Mahwah, NJ: Lawrence Erlbaum Associates, 2003); M. Gail Jones, Brett D. Jones, and Tracy Y. Hargrove, *The unintended consequences of high-stakes testing* (Lanham, MD: Rowman & Littlefield, 2003); Neumann, "Examining mandated testing, teachers' milieu, *and* teachers' knowledge and beliefs," *Teachers College Record* 118, no. 2 (February 2016): 1–50; and Cynthia Salinas, "Teaching in a high-stakes testing setting," in *Measuring history: Cases of state-level testing across the United States*, ed. S. G. Grant (Charlotte, NC: Information Age Publishing, 2006), 177–93.

13. Neumann, "Examining mandated testing," 1–50.

14. Jacob Fischler, "What parents need to know about school vouchers," *U.S. News & World Report*, October 22, 2021, https://www.usnews.com/education/k12/articles/what-parents-need-to-know-about-school-vouchers.

15. David Tyack and William Tobin, "The 'grammar' of schooling: Why has it been so hard to change?" *American Education Research Journal* 31, no. 3 (1994): 454.

16. David Tyack and Larry Cuban, *Tinkering toward utopia: A century of public school reform* (Cambridge, MA: Harvard University Press, 1995), 85.

17. One-room schoolhouses were inefficient and hard to manage. The idea of all the six-year-olds being put in first grade, the seven-year-olds in second grade, the eight-year-olds in third grade, and so on made such common sense that the idea quickly spread. Carnegie units provided a similar type of organization, although for subject matter instead of age. Prior to 1900, colleges as well as high schools were unorganized, with little to identify them as part of the same type of school. Carnegie units started as a way for elite colleges to organize and separate themselves, giving structure through systematizing the way content was taught and accounted for. Accrediting agencies and high schools quickly followed suit because they wanted to be recognized as having high quality. For a more thorough history of these two reforms, see Tyack and Cuban, *Tinkering toward utopia*.

18. Metz, "Real school," 75–91.

19. Reid, "Curriculum as institutionalized learning," 34.

20. Larry Cuban, "Constancy and change in schools (1880s to the present)," in *Contributing to educational change: Perspectives on research and practice*, ed. Philip W. Jackson (Berkeley, CA: McCutchan Publishing Company, 1988), 85–105.

21. This might not apply to all first-order changes, however. Increasing teacher salaries would be a first-order change, but because it might cost taxpayers more in taxes, such a change might require public support.

22. Jonathan G. Silin and Fran Schwartz, "Staying close to the teacher," *Teachers College Record* 105, no. 8 (October 2003): 1586.

23. Joseph J. Schwab, "The practical 4: Something for curriculum professors to do," *Curriculum Inquiry* 13, no. 3 (1983): 241.

24. Mary M. Kennedy, "Knowledge and vision in teaching," *Journal of Teacher Education* 57, no. 3 (May 2006): 206.

25. Tyack and Cuban, *Tinkering toward utopia*, 65.

26. Tyack and Cuban, *Tinkering toward utopia.*

Chapter 8

Work *with* Power to Maximize Students' Learning

You've now seen individual arguments and lessons about power across multiple contexts in schools and with students, teachers, and school leaders. This chapter ends the book by shifting focus and presenting collective suggestions for using power to maximize students' learning. How you understand and act on power either makes learning easier and more effective, or it makes learning more complicated and less efficient.

Unfortunately, because most people get power in schools wrong, many schools don't run as effectively as they could. Even if the school and central administration always try to "move forward" (even if myopically at times), pursuing goals such as high-accountability ratings, the school likely wastes time and doesn't maximize its resources: teachers juggle too many competing demands, people have to backtrack on decisions, instructional time gets wasted, and more.

These problems might seem logistical, a result of inadequate training, or as just the way schools are. They're not. Many boil down to how people think about power. If, say, people only think that power flows downhill or that only certain people held power, then it's not important to consider how students or teachers can use their own power over a situation, because they might not have power to exert. When people think that "big" power impacts schools more than "small" power, there's no need to worry about how schools will assimilate reforms. If students hold no power, then ascertaining their thinking about issues will be simple.

Faulty thinking causes people to look at the wrong things as making the biggest impacts on schools. For example, people tend to fixate on the power of standardized testing, legislation, and school reform efforts. Or they worry too much about the next political test, such as protesting students or angry parents. Those are certainly important; there's no denying the impact they make on schools. But the evidence suggests that the small stuff makes just as much—and perhaps more—impact on schools than big public attempts to change schools. Plus, and this is crucial, the small stuff never stops. It doesn't trend. In a real sense, the small stuff is relentless.

The small stuff emphasizes the daily operations of schools and classrooms and is largely hidden from public view. You saw examples of small stuff throughout chapters 3–6, such as teachers changing the curriculum, principals issuing initiatives and making personnel decisions, and students voicing contradicting opinions. However, the small stuff is not small in its practical effects. Indeed, it points a way forward for improving schools—they're not big, they don't try to completely rethink schooling à la second-order change. They won't make the news.

Last, faulty thinking about power causes people to think that powerful people and events ultimately shape how schooling operates and, thus, to think that power is something to be wielded, fought, or avoided (à la Machiavelli). As a result, schools often do not maximize their teachers' effectiveness. Schools often unnecessarily complicate teachers' work. They often focus on legislation, on mandates, and on the political climate. They impose top-down fixes that *always* get revised when implemented in classrooms. And they seldom exhibit the humility needed to make necessary changes.

Schools don't try to mess up students' learning, of course. Test prep demands, paperwork, assessment structures, and the like often result from schools' attempts to improve learning. Yet those measures too often end up acting as obstacles to teachers' power to create meaningful learning for students. Orlando Gaines described their impact on his own thinking about school: "I used to be driving to school, and I'd be thinking about curriculum. I'd be thinking about history. I'd be thinking about what I'm doing that day. Now I drive to school and think, What have I not turned in? What are we behind in? It's always about that."

The previous chapters showed many examples of schools working against power. Tomas's story in chapter 6 provides one example. Tomas was a new principal at the time, so he couldn't reasonably be expected to predict that outcome. But his assistant superintendent wasn't new. If that assistant superintendent had recognized that power works as a web, maybe she would have predicted that string of events and worked to avoid wasting Tomas's time on it.

Another example is the grading tension between the school district scope and sequence and the IB program that was described in chapter 4. When teachers engage in that kind of balancing act, they don't maximize their time and abilities. Apparently, nobody in the central office understood the power exerted by both grading systems, so nobody helped teachers to develop a process for managing that tension. Here, district administrators worked against the power of the teachers to use their time well when they did not help the teachers to remedy the problem.

Accurate thinking about power in schools, on the other hand, helps maximize student learning. This thinking recognizes the factors that most shape schooling, and it isn't distracted by things merely attracting the most public attention. It maximizes teachers' time, knowledge, and experience. It understands the contingent nature of authority, that nobody makes decisions without consequences, especially unintended ones. Plus, this thinking recognizes that power always exists in schools. It understands that power is an inevitable by-product of the free association of people working in a shared enterprise and, as such, can only be navigated.

So how does correct thinking about power help people to work *with* and not *against* power? To answer this question, first consider a school's goals. Most schools make school ratings their top priority, such as the A–F rating system in Texas. That's a mistake. The main goal for any school system should be to maximize the effectiveness of its teachers and staff. Maximizing a staff's effectiveness makes it easier to earn high ratings and engage students in meaningful learning, as well as generate other benefits for students.

This might seem like a contradiction or perhaps even fortune cookie advice: to maximize student learning, a school shouldn't focus on student learning but should focus on teachers' effectiveness. How can that be right? Think about it like this. If the main goal focuses on students, then school leaders might feel tempted to exert more power (through initiatives, directives, programs, etc.), which blocks or diminishes the power that teachers are able to exert over their teaching. You've seen how that approach can cause unintended problems.

But if the focus is on teachers' effectiveness, leaders should try to *remove* obstacles to teachers' maximum effectiveness. Removing obstacles can help teachers to perform better, to use their power more efficiently and productively, which can help students learn more. That means reducing unnecessary distractions, paperwork, and impositions that teachers have to navigate so that they can spend as much mental time and energy on their teaching. In real terms, that's the best leaders can do in terms of power if they want schools to run optimally. Leaders can opt for more action/reaction approaches, but you've seen how inefficient those approaches often are.

This is what is meant, then, by working with power: helping teachers to develop, direct, and channel their power to enhance students' learning. This doesn't ask school leaders to share power. Leaders already do that, whether they recognize it or not. Since the web of power can't be willed or forced away, leaders should embrace the power network, understand how it works, and use it to maximize teachers' effectiveness. The best teachers are always exerting power to create meaningful learning for students. So do the best principals and superintendents. The goal is for those power influences to work with each other and not against each other.

But don't schools do this already? Some do, but too many do not—or at least not well enough. Too many schools take away weeks of instructional days from teachers for benchmark testing that shuts down the schools, sometimes up to fifteen days of testing across a year, which equals three weeks of testing! Too many schools burden teachers with paperwork and administrative duties so that they cause teachers to worry like Orlando about regulations instead of about teaching. Too many schools impose practices and policies onto teachers without engaging them in productive conversations about what best practices might mean for them.

Further, too many people in schools think about teaching as a form of technology, what the education scholar Elliot Eisner calls "curriculum as technology."[1] This is not computer technology, mind you. Rather, it is teaching as a tool to achieve a goal. The goal is usually to meet the standards and do well on the tests. Curriculum and teaching, when considered as tools, get designed to reach goals as efficiently as possible. Efficiency isn't bad. It can be essential, in fact. But a myopic focus on efficiency for the sake of test scores crowds out more meaningful inquiry and learning.

Acting with power doesn't imply making bold, public changes, the kind that Larry Cuban calls "second-order" changes, which is good, because, according to the scholar Mary Kennedy, "not only are bold ideas likely to fail, they also are likely to hinder our progress toward real improvement by distracting educators and making it more difficult for them to concentrate."[2] Instead, these suggestions emphasize first-order changes. These are changes within existing school systems that make the systems run better for teachers and students.

This is no simple task, though. First, one has to recognize that a school staff's effectiveness probably *isn't* maximized and that school policies and structures are likely a big cause. And second, one must be willing to eliminate or revise conditions that impede their effectiveness, which likely means changing school policies or practices. Further, tackling these problems requires confronting a sort of paradox: the routines, beliefs, and modes of operating that make schools manageable simultaneously restrict their effectiveness.

Schools utilize routines. In fact, schools couldn't operate without them, because routines help schools turn inherently unstable environments into predictable and useful places to learn.[3] Because routines are so essential to a school's daily functioning, teachers and school leaders can become possessive of them. When threatened, this possessiveness can breed what's called *threat rigidity*. If organizations feel themselves under siege, they often respond in predictable ways: centralized control increases, conformity is stressed, accountability is emphasized, and innovating thinking is discouraged.[4]

Hence the paradox: particular routines and modes of being help schools function, but they also limit their effectiveness. Accurately recognizing and addressing power requires rethinking particular routines and modes of being, but doing so isn't easy, since calls for change can increase the rigidity of those routines. Strong leadership at all levels becomes crucial for teachers, principals, superintendents, and other school leaders to work together toward change.

FIVE ESSENTIAL ACTIONS THAT WORK *WITH* POWER

Toward this end, this book concludes by suggesting five actions that can help schools work *with* power instead of against it. These suggestions are simple, but they're not easy. They likely won't be popular either, because they cut against typical ways of running schools and classrooms. These suggestions emphasize leading from the back rather than from the front. Leading from the front aligns with action/reaction thinking about power. Leading from the front can create results. Leaders can teach new attitudes, practices, and beliefs, inspiring them and providing a path for them to follow. They can implement a plan and hold others accountable to it.

Too often, though, school leaders lead only from the front. Too often they only emphasize power as action/reaction. Too often they act too much and don't listen enough. To maximize student learning, however, school leaders need to incorporate more leading from the back. This might sound counterintuitive. After all, the historical model is one of a teacher up in front of a classroom, a principal up in front of a school, and a superintendent up in front of a school district.

But schools need more of this style of leadership. Leading from the back aligns with thinking about power as a web. The leader follows behind the others, in a sense, and tries to develop others' power and competence. Nelson Mandela, in his autobiography *Long Walk to Freedom*, describes leadership in terms of a shepherd walking behind the flock, always letting the weakest go ahead, sometimes redirecting, sometimes nudging, and sometimes protecting from danger.[5]

Teachers can benefit from all of these suggestions, but they're really directed more at school leaders—and especially at superintendents since superintendents set the tone for accountability and standards in a school district, not just for ratings purposes but—and more importantly—for inquiry into problems and integrity in addressing problems. More so than teachers, school leaders have the ability to promote within a school and across schools a working with power instead of working against power.

1. Get Ego Out of the Way

Think of a school or school district. Perhaps it's yours. Do principals, teachers, and superintendents value and search for truth, regardless of where that truth comes from? Can all faculty, staff, and administrators publicly—and constructively—criticize each other equally in the search for the best ideas? Can, say, a teacher stand up in a faculty meeting and point out potential flaws in a principal's plan for implementing a new program? In a meeting with principals and an assistant superintendent, can a principal publicly make suggestions to improve a district policy? If not, why is that?

Feedback among school personnel that is constrained, that is opaque, and that is less than fully honest will not facilitate truth seeking. It will not facilitate finding the best answers to problems; instead, it will likely cause problems. For example, the school will be continuously susceptible to the "fundamental attribution error,"[6] which means that, when searching for the causes of people's behavior, too much value is placed on a person's character and not enough is placed on the contexts within which the behavior occurred. In other words, people will misread situations.

Opaque decision making can also create what Mary Kennedy calls "reform clutter."[7] Simply put, too many school improvement plans operating simultaneously can "clutter" teaching, get in the teachers' way, and negate the effects of each other.[8] Trust can also be a casualty of opaque communication. Indeed, one researcher found a high degree of distrust directed at teachers by principals and parents.[9] Principals can similarly feel distrust from the central office or from teachers.

Do any organizations operate with high levels of honesty and openness? There are a few. One example is Bridgewater, a hedge fund founded by Ray Dalio in the mid-1970s. Bridgewater eventually became the most successful and influential hedge fund in the world. In 2016 *Fortune* magazine named Bridgewater the fifth most important private company in the US. Now, schools aren't hedge funds, of course, but the principles Dalio shares from his experience building Bridgewater hold useful lessons for educators . . . if they have the courage to listen.[10]

At Bridgewater, Dalio created what he calls an idea meritocracy. Dalio claims that "there is no better way to make decisions than to have believable people open-mindedly and assertively surface, explore, and resolve their differences."[11] Bridgewater built this idea meritocracy by practicing five principles: radical truth, radical transparency, radical open-mindedness, recognizing people's barriers, and believability weighting.

Radical truth is simple: don't filter your thoughts—say exactly what you think. But it isn't easy to practice. At Bridgewater no one's actions or decisions, not even the CEO's, are above public scrutiny, because scrutiny produces better decisions. Do school leaders do this? Do they invite critique by subordinates? Do they put out their ideas for review? Do they publicly admit what they don't know and seek advice from others? If the CEO of the largest hedge fund in the world can do this, why not a superintendent or a school principal? For Dalio, the best leaders focus entirely on results, not on image or on being right.

Radical transparency means "giving most everyone the ability to see most everything."[12] Every decision at Bridgewater is made with as much transparency as possible because resentment can breed when employees don't know the reasoning behind decision making. Apply this to schools. School leaders make tough decisions, such as moving staff from one school to another, allocating resources, prioritizing funding, and more. In these decisions, are the impacted staff included in the decision-making process? According to Dalio, this increases trust and optimizes insights that others bring to a decision.

Radical open-mindedness means that, because nobody knows everything, everyone needs to become accustomed to finding truth in unexpected sources, which is the only way to make the best decisions possible. Apply this to schools. Is a leader's job to provide answers or to find the best answers, regardless of where they are found? Leaders navigate multiple challenges. But what about the leader who makes decisions in isolation, decisions that impact teachers and staff, even when all agree that nobody knows everything? Might that leader be missing insight from other people? How can the leader know her answer is the best if it isn't stress tested in advance?

Everyone has barriers. Dalio focuses on two: the "ego barrier" and the "blind spot barrier"; these two barriers "make it difficult for you to objectively see what is true about you and your circumstances and to make the best possible decisions by getting the most out of others."[13] The ego barrier makes it hard for us to accept our mistakes and weaknesses, and the blind spot barrier prevents us from seeing things clearly. Things go badly when people don't acknowledge their blind spots. Often, angry disagreements ensue when people don't recognize they might be wrong and that the other person might be right.

Everybody's thoughts need to be heard. But not everybody's opinions are equally believable. Take baseball. Which suggestions about hitting are more valid: those from a repeat batting champion or from a rookie? This doesn't mean that one can't learn from a rookie. It means that the opinions of the batting champion have more believability. Dalio argues that "the best decisions are made by an idea meritocracy with believability-weighted decision making, in which the most capable people work through disagreements with other capable people who have thought independently about what is true and what to do about it."[14]

If school leaders have the courage to promote radical truth and transparency, then they need to engage the most believable staff in working through important issues. Say math scores have been low in an elementary school. Does the school district impose yet another "solution" on the teachers in the school? Does the principal find another "fix" in terms of professional development? Or does the leadership share the nature of the problem in full transparency; gather together the faculty with the most experience, the most believability in teaching math; and together work through the problem until the best answer can be found?

Of the many challenges employees face at Bridgewater, getting their ego out of the way is key. In a collaborative venture such as a hedge fund, ego merely impedes the search for the best answers. Dalio writes that over one-third of newly hired employees at Bridgewater quit within the first few months because they can't handle radical truth (Bridgewater plans for this, building this winnowing process into their hiring plans). Likely, the new employees who quit let their egos get in the way. Bridgewater sees this winnowing process as necessary to the company's long-term success.

The same goes for schools. Schools of course don't want one-third of new teachers to quit. But it's useful to recognize that ego limits people's ability to access truth because their ego doesn't want to hear criticism. But growth requires criticism because people don't know everything and they make mistakes. Abandoning ego also works *with* power. It understands that as people exercise their power, they add more to the task. Indeed, abandoning ego invites teachers and school leaders at all levels to more fully and honestly contribute to the search for truth.

2. Collaboratively Address "System-Level Problems"

At first glance, helping teachers teach to their strengths seems straightforward—provide them with useful professional development, classroom resources, and time to plan as a team. Maybe give them a couple more special provisions depending on context or the subject being taught, but that's about it. Or so the thinking goes. Those problems aren't easy, of course. What makes professional development (PD) useful? Can you even find useful PD? Resources cost money. Can you afford them? How much planning time is optimal . . . or possible? Is it forty-five-minute blocks several times a week, or maybe one two-hour block once a week?

Call these *classroom-level problems*. Addressing classroom-level problems is standard practice for schools trying to improve teaching effectiveness. For example, teachers learn new planning and teaching methods (i.e., 5E lesson planning or teaching with inquiry); schools buy new technology such as tablets, computer labs, or smartboards; schools change how teachers teach reading (i.e., more or less phonics, whether to use sustained silent reading, interactive notebooks); and more.

However, these aren't the only problems that keep teachers from teaching to their strengths. For example, what obstacles get in teachers' way from doing their best teaching? Are those obstacles structural? Are they procedural? What distractions divert teachers' attention away from teaching? What teaching methods and practices get imposed onto teachers by school leaders? Do they help or hinder teachers' teaching? How do you know? How much teaching time do teachers lose to assessment related to high-stakes testing? Are there other ways to conduct that assessment and *not* lose so much instructional time? Call this second set *system-level problems*.

Classroom-level problems focus on issues and decisions located mainly inside classrooms. System-level problems, on the other hand, involve policies that originate from school leaders, especially superintendents. System-level problems receive far less public attention than classroom-level problems. Well, teachers understand the problem of losing instructional time to assessment. They understand the problem of having to incorporate assorted and sometimes random programs and initiatives into their teaching. They understand the problem of paperwork, such as you saw in chapter 5 with the homework initiative.

But teachers and school leaders rarely work together to resolve system-level problems or to make them less of an obstacle to teachers. Much more often, policies and programs flow down "the conduit," a sort of policy pipeline which funnels directives from school leaders down onto teachers in classrooms.[15] In a real sense, classroom-level problems are the only problems eligible for public and collegial deliberation inside schools; system-level problems seem untouchable and off-limits to public debate. They can hugely impact teachers' effectiveness, but teachers are allowed no input into them.

Why is this? Power seems to play a role. School leaders often lead from the front, which aligns with action/reaction thinking about power. Here power is thought to flow from leaders down to teachers and staff. This stance certainly doesn't understand that power works like a web. Is it also about ego? Do school leaders think they'll be seen as less effective if their opinions are publicly questioned? Do they worry about looking weak? Do they just not want their judgment questioned by employees? Or do they think teachers don't have the expertise to deliberate on such problems?

Classroom-level problems warrant careful thought. But if schools are ever to maximize teachers' teaching effectiveness—and thereby maximize students' learning—they must rethink their practices regarding system-level problems. Change, though, has to start at the top. Principals can invite teachers into a collaborative process. But they can't buck central office policies on testing. They can't refuse to implement the teaching practices on their campuses that an assistant superintendent gives them. Superintendents hold the real power to foster collaboration, perhaps most importantly by setting a collaborative tone and example for the school district.

So how might school leaders collectively address system-level problems to help teachers teach to their strengths? The basic answer is simple: superintendents and other school leaders need to lead from the rear more often and invite more people into system-level decision-making processes. Schools and school districts don't need to be direct democracies, and scale is a problem. Maybe, then, convene an advisory task force of teachers from around the district. For some decisions, maybe just department chairs or team leaders participate, and those teachers can bring feedback to and from other teachers. Maybe include more teachers for other decisions.

What specific system-level problems might school leaders collaborate on with teachers? Try these: (1) balancing instructional time with assessment and other preparation for high-stakes testing, (2) imposing teaching practices onto teachers, (3) creating paperwork demands on teachers, and (4) enforcing a rigid pacing calendar. Each problem generates obstacles to teachers' effectiveness. Each works against teachers' power inside their classrooms. And teachers know them well since teachers have to live with them every day in their work.

It's possible, of course, that school leaders don't consider these issues to be problems. These issues are likely considered necessary steps in producing high test scores. After all, pacing mandates, which require teachers to be at specific points in their content by specific dates, help ensure teachers get through all of the content in time for the test. Benchmarking helps schools assess students' learning as they progress toward testing. Requiring teachers to include particular teaching methods helps principals ensure that students experience desired learning modalities. And paperwork is just a byproduct of documenting various school actions.

However, teachers can experience these issues very differently. Regarding the pacing problem, for example, Margaret normally taught about Andrew Jackson in early February. She moved slowly in the beginning of the school year to establish a conceptual foundation with the English Civil War and took time to help students make visceral connections through what she called "act it outs," dramatic engagements with the content. She moved faster through later content to catch up by late March, in plenty of time for testing. She knew from her over three decades of teaching experience that her system worked well, and her students earned the test scores to support it.

But new pacing mandates required her to teach about Jackson in mid-January, limiting her time to build that foundation and engage in act it outs. One might think, "What's the big deal? It's only two weeks." The problem is that Margaret couldn't build that foundation as well as she previously could, plus she had to eliminate multiple act it outs, such as for Washington crossing the Delaware. Despite its intentions, the pacing calendar worked against Margaret's power to create the most effective learning for her students. It limited Margaret's creativity, but more importantly, it limited students' opportunities to deeply learn about important issues.

Or take the habit of imposing teaching practices onto teachers. You saw examples of this in chapter 5. School leaders mean well when they do this—it's done to improve teaching in the school, the quality of which is ultimately their responsibility. Yet the evidence suggests that teachers are more likely to take those initiatives negatively. Teachers have good reasons to act protectively toward their teaching. Practices which might be "best" abstractly or in other contexts are always evaluated through the lens of "what works" in those teachers' classes. Thus, imposed practices are evaluated through that skeptical lens.

This distinction between classroom-level and system-level problems isn't entirely new. A practice called "systems thinking" was developed in 1951,[16] and it has been linked to education for at least thirty years.[17] Systems thinking tries to look holistically at education. It asks, for example, how cuts in one area of school—say, in music education—impact other areas, such as in language teaching. It embraces a "many-to-one" perspective, in which students can access many sources of information, only one of which is the teacher.[18] Systems thinking has influenced teaching fields such as geography, chemistry, nursing, and agriculture.[19]

However, like most efforts at improving schools, this notion of systems thinking also suffers from power imbalances. It's been argued that leaders in human systems such as education can create meaningful change by developing climates of trust, mutual respect, and innovation. But to do this, it's claimed, leaders will need to share control with "group/system members,"[20] which is a problem since power inequalities lead to disconnection between reform planners and implementers.[21]

In practice, however, system-thinking paradigms too often maintain the strict division between classroom- and system-level problems. School leaders seldom invite teachers and other staff to deliberate on system-level problems. Foregrounding power into those conversations highlights the necessity of valuing multiple insights into problems. It's not effective for leaders to restrict teachers from publicly considering and debating some of their most pressing problems. System-level problems can seriously disrupt teachers' classrooms, and schools need all the insight, creativity, and understanding that can be brought to bear on them.

3. Recognize That You're Bad at Predicting the Future, but Try to Do It Anyway

School leaders never intend to cause problems in their schools. But it happens. How do administrators address problems or perceived deficiencies within schools? Often they implement new programs or initiatives targeted at the problems. The trouble is that programs and initiatives don't start with a blank slate. They don't exist inside a vacuum. They don't act on only one problem. Instead, they are introduced into a web of other initiatives, influences, and factors that all tug on each other, all exerting power on each other, creating ripples across teachers' work, school policies, and professional relationships that can create as many problems as they solve.

You saw examples of this in chapter 5. Remember the instructional rounds that Orlando Gaines, in his colorful language, called a "pain in the ass?" In a vacuum, doing instructional rounds is probably always a productive and useful practice. But in that particular context at Connors, what those teachers experienced most was the burden of extra paperwork. The intent was to help teachers develop their craft. The lived effect, unfortunately, was yet another task to complete for the administration.

This isn't to disparage instructional rounds. Perhaps the implementation at Connors could have been different—more generative and collegial than burdensome. Perhaps teachers could have been simply encouraged to watch each other teach—and provided someone to briefly cover their classes instead of having to use their planning or conference time. Perhaps the paperwork could have been eliminated. Perhaps an administrator could have arranged to join a team meeting to learn what the team gained from the experiences—and to share in the conversation as a colleague.

Why were instructional rounds not a success for these teachers at Connors when they easily could have been? It was probably because the administration didn't try to predict the future. They didn't foresee how their particular implementation might interact with teachers' feelings of stress, of lack of time, and maybe even of feeling surveilled by paperwork and reporting on each other's work. In short, they didn't foresee the power of all of the other influences on the teachers' work and how those influences would interact with and impact this new initiative.

How could administrators have known about teachers' stress or about teachers' worries over time? They could have asked. Understanding the web nature of power, administrators could have asked, say, department chairs how they thought teachers might react to an instructional rounds initiative and how it might be most productively implemented and then analyzed. Would administrators merely follow the teachers' suggestions? Of course not. The process would be a collaboration between mostly equal partners. The administration communicates their goals and seeks input from teachers on the best way to enact the program.

Or maybe the administration could have already developed and maintained such close communication with teams, department chairs, and teachers that they were already in tune with teachers' stresses and worries. This approach would require close collaboration and communication throughout a school year. It would require relating to teachers as partners in a shared endeavor with a shared goal—but not the goal of high test scores—instead, the goal of maximizing teachers' and the school's effectiveness. It would recognize and appreciate that principals *share* power with teachers.

This analysis applies to superintendents as well. Don't just dictate to principals. Instead, tell them goals and work with them to discover the most effective processes for achieving those goals. After all, principals know their campuses far better than does the central office. Many teachers already practice this with their students. They'll tell students their goals and work with them to figure out how to make them happen. These teachers understand and respect that both they *and* their students exert power in the classroom, and they choose to work with that power instead of against it. Superintendents should do that too—not occasionally but consistently.

Now step back and try to predict the potential outcomes of more actions: the personnel and course-management decisions like you saw in chapter 6, all kinds of program and initiative decisions like you saw in chapter 5, curriculum decisions, and professional development decisions. In pretty much every decision in running schools and classrooms, think about how the people involved exert power and how that power might interact with your program, initiative, or decision. Maintain collaboration and an attitude toward power that facilitates this type of relationship. And if in doubt, talk with the other people involved about it.

Occasionally, you'll guess right; you saw how Lionel Avila correctly predicted his personnel decision. You won't always predict the future correctly, of course. You won't always discern precisely how a program or initiative will play out within the school's milieu. Ego can't get in the way, though, because this is usually not a solitary task. It's usually not a leader's job to divine the future from a lonely office (firing decisions like Lionel's might be an exception). But usually, collaboration and relationship will be key, so make predicting the future a team effort. If you want to maximize teachers' effectiveness, you have to try.

4. Help Teachers Teach to Their Strengths

Teachers should teach to their strengths. That seems commonsensical enough. But what does it mean? In practice the answer is simple: teach in ways that generate the most learning for students. Teaching to strengths is not the same as using "best practices." "Best practices" are touted as universal, but research by this author finds that best practices depend on context and students' needs.[22] So best practices can be an imposition, just like anything else. This includes so called high-leverage practices. Best practices and high-leverage practices aren't bad; they can be quite useful. But they're a different thing from teaching to one's strengths.

Teaching to strengths means knowing how you're most effective when teaching. It means using your power not to impose it onto students like a tyrant but to creatively generate the most meaningful thinking and learning that you can. It means being aware of a range of possible ways to teach and using the approach that best suits your temper, intellect, skills, patience, and interest. It means knowing how to artfully match techniques and processes with the needs of the context at hand. But it doesn't mean uniformity, since teachers likely won't have the same strengths, even if they teach the same subject in the same grade level.

Contrast Margaret's and Bill's classrooms. Both taught eighth-grade US history. They taught differently but were equally effective. Margaret told stories in her teaching. When introducing and taking students through content, she, you might say, lectured in a storytelling format. Bill, on the other hand, mainly asked questions to students. You might call it a Socratic-type method. Bill didn't lecture; he used questions to lead students through content. The processes were different, but each helped students to make deep connections with and remember content many months later.

Connors was lucky because Mary, Bill, Margaret, and Orlando all taught to their strengths. They each had many years of experience—over thirty years each for Margaret and Mary—and they all knew precisely why they used particular methods and how those methods impacted their students. They knew what they were good at and what they weren't good at. *However, it's not clear that all or even most teachers teach to their strengths.* New teachers, teachers who struggle, and teachers who can't reflect deeply on their specific teaching practices and the reasons for them all likely don't teach to their strengths.

This is a problem because teachers can't teach their best unless they know what their best is. It's also a tough problem to solve. For starters, how can teachers know how they best teach? Veteran teachers might have experimented enough and done enough trial and error to figure out how they teach best. New and early career teachers, however, likely don't have enough repetition to determine that quickly. It's been known for a long time that most teachers teach like they were taught. This is especially true for new and early career teachers.

A big reason for this is what's called the "apprenticeship of observation."[23] Most people are students for at least twelve years (first to twelfth grades). Add a year for kindergarten. Teachers are students for at least sixteen years, even more if they attended preschool and graduate school. That's a lot of years to apprentice by watching teachers teach. That's a lot of time to learn what it means to be a "real" teacher.[24] Those lessons stick. In fact, they form ways of thinking about teaching that are hard to break.

Research on teacher education supports this insight. It's unclear how strong the effects of teacher education are on how new teachers teach. Many studies suggest that teacher education programs don't change how teacher candidates think about teaching. In effect, some research says that students enter teacher preparation programs with particular ways of thinking about teaching, they learn new teaching and assessment strategies, and then they graduate with those original beliefs bolstered by some newly gained skills. All of this implies that new teachers often enter teaching knowing how other people teach but not how *they* teach best.

This isn't to criticize teacher preparation programs. Just helping students to become certified to teach can be a huge feat. But it does highlight the problem: where can teachers learn how they teach best? It is not in teacher preparation programs nor through school-provided professional development; those programs usually just introduce teachers to new programs and practices, which teachers then compare to their current practices. It is also not through most school-based mentoring programs.

If none of these common programs and practices help teachers learn to teach to their strengths, how and where can teachers learn this? Experience can help; in fact, that's usually the only way that teachers learn their strengths. Repetition, mindful trial and error, and continuous reflection can help teachers figure out their strengths. Donald Schön calls this process "reflective practice" in which professionals make sense in real time how they make decisions within the daily, lived contexts of their work.[25] But it doesn't benefit schools to wait so long for teachers to figure out on their own how they teach best, if they figure it out at all.

Instead, schools should make it a priority to help teachers learn their strengths. Doing so will take concerted effort and a wise use of power, but the process can be blended into the normal operating functions of the school from onboarding and mentoring to faculty meetings and professional development. State-level teacher evaluation systems may already support such a focus. In Texas, for example, the Texas Teacher Evaluation and Support System (T-TESS) includes a section for teacher self-assessment. In this section, teachers and school leaders can work together to focus on teacher strengths and weaknesses.

You may wonder if school evaluation systems already emphasize teachers' strengths. They do somewhat but not to the extent or in the manner necessary. Current processes are usually individual, private, between a teacher and administrator, and strictly for evaluation purposes. They aren't addressed in public. In contrast, schools need an open, public process. Not that teachers' evaluations should be made public. Rather, school leaders should position the development of teachers' strengths as a prime action for the school, something to be collegially discussed and shared.

How could this work? For starters, school leaders could bring it up during faculty meetings, even by asking something simple such as "What does it mean for us to teach to our strengths? How can we know if we are?" The school leader could make this a public goal and problem that faculty should work toward—again, not in a manner that suggests faculty lack ability but as a way of continuously improving teaching at the school.

The school would need to develop a system through which teachers would try different teaching methods; the school would determine how to assess those methods; and then, over time, the staff would debrief and analyze their success. That's it: try a method over time, evaluate its success, and talk about how the teachers felt when using it. Schools already do this to some degree. But usually it's handled as something to merely show teachers and then assumed that they will figure out on their own if and how to incorporate the new methods into their teaching. This suggestion makes that basic practice more intense, more thorough, and more formal.

Say that math teachers in a school typically lectured and used document cameras to demonstrate concepts to students. That is pretty typical. Someone could work with them on using inquiry or Socratic-type questioning. The math department and school leaders could collaborate over a period of time. They'd have to determine what success means. And they'd need to help teachers analyze both the success of the method and the teachers' feeling of self-efficacy. Over time teachers could be helped with incorporating some or all of the new method into their teaching. Who picks the methods to try? Both teachers and school leaders do. It's a collaboration.

The point isn't to criticize or impose on teachers but to collectively develop their power to create meaningful learning for students. And leaders would need to develop and use their power to help teachers learn. Teachers shouldn't be forced to use particular methods. Leaders shouldn't say, "Here's a method I want to see in your teaching." The process should focus on public and mindful continuous improvement. Perhaps the biggest obstacles will be in shifting the school's mindset from one of evaluation to one of collaboration, in guarding one's teaching practices from public discussion, and in sharing responsibility for teaching in the school.

5. Do School *with* Students and Families and Not *to* Students and Families

Schools relate to students and families in one of two broad ways: they either do school *with* students and families, or they do school *to* students and families. The approach teachers and school leaders pick reflects, in part, how they think about power. To do school *with* students and families recognizes the web of power. It recognizes that students and families, just like teachers and school leaders, will also exert power on schooling situations. This approach helps maximize students' learning. It doesn't put unnecessary obstacles in the way of students' learning. It works with students and families to create the most effective and meaningful learning for students.

To do school *to* students and families, on the other hand, does not maximize students' learning. It hinders learning. It says that teachers and school leaders know better than families about what's best for students. It imposes ideologies and agendas onto students. Oftentimes, when families and students make clear that they don't want those ideologies, teachers and school leaders don't back down. In some extreme cases, parents have been locked out of school board meetings, and protesting parents have been arrested at their homes by school district police.[26]

Even without the ideology, even when just focused on the nuts and bolts of learning, families and school personnel find collaboration can still present challenges. In working with parents and families, teachers and principals have always had to negotiate a balance among sometimes-competing influences: state curriculum; school culture, protocols, and programs; teachers' goals; and parents' wishes. Notice the web of power embedded within this dialectic? Each of those influences exerts power, tugging on this activity called "schooling" and impacting students' learning. The trick is to align the tugs in such a way as to maximize students' learning.

In practice schools don't typically follow just one way of relating to parents and families. They typically do a mix of both. Sometimes they collaborate; other times, they impose. To help maximize students' learning, schools should collaborate more than they impose. They should do school *with* students and families more than they do school *to* them—a lot more. The research is clear on this: collaboration produces more buy in, more support, and more participation from families. Collaboration helps teachers and families remove or work around obstacles. Imposition, in contrast, creates obstacles that limit learning.

Collaboration seems easy to understand and do. Teachers and families work together to identify and solve problems. Teachers create open and multiple lines of communication, and they can meet with parents in person, online, or on the phone to discuss progress. Teachers can share diagnostic and formative data. Parents can share students' learning history, strengths, and weaknesses as far as they understand them. Teachers can share what learning looks like in the classroom. Teachers and parents can discuss how they can best work together to reach goals.

Sometimes parents know how to exercise their power to enhance their children's learning. Maybe they already read to their children or practice math skills with them. In those cases, teachers can simply request that parents and families work on particular skills, such as sight words for primary students or more advanced writing skills for high school students. Those cases are ideal, but they do exist. Teachers just need to utilize parents and families as teaching partners.

In other cases, teachers may need to train parents and families on how to best help their children. The parents may be willing and wanting to help their children learn, but perhaps they lack the teaching skills. Teachers can provide resources, such as reading or math workbooks, and show parents how to do simple, short (say, ten-minute) practices exercises with their children. Or say parents want to help but feel they haven't the time. Maybe teachers can show them how to keep updated about their children's progress, perhaps using school databases such as Skyward. In all of these examples, teachers just have to figure out how to best help parents help their kids.

That's the classroom level. What about system-level collaboration? Well, just like teachers are usually left out of system-level issues, so too are parents and families. Usually these issues are just imposed on teachers and parents alike. But is collaboration possible with parents and families on system-level issues? Yes, and it is mainly in the form of gathering feedback related to policies, programs, and initiatives.

Instead of only telling parents and families what the new policies are, school leaders could host feedback opportunities related to, say, proposed homework policies, laptop programs, or new writing-across-the-curriculum initiatives. They could use online survey instruments such as Qualtrics or Survey Monkey to gather feedback from parents, as well as schedule in-person meetings to listen to parents and families.

OK. So far so good. You may already know these tips, or perhaps they're simply useful reminders. But what about impositions? The typical imposition occurs when a school or teacher announces a new curriculum policy or program without gathering feedback from parents and families, such as those mentioned in the previous paragraphs. But what about, say, a benchmark testing schedule? Could parents help with that? Likely not, since they likely have no experience or expertise to draw from in giving feedback, nor are they negatively impacted one way or another by a testing schedule.

So some topics can benefit from parent and family input, such as school-wide homework policies, but other topics likely provide little benefit, such as benchmark testing policies. In this example, the latter remains an imposition, but the imposition is reasonable and justified. What's the criteria, then, for deciding whether an imposition is reasonable? Two criteria seem important. First, can parent input potentially improve the policy, program, or initiative? Second, can parents and families be significantly or meaningfully impacted by the policy, program, or initiative?

Following this logic, parents and families might improve a school-wide homework policy since they can speak to the impact the policy might have inside households. But they likely can't improve and aren't impacted by a benchmark testing schedule. Apply these two tests to other issues. What about with dress code or uniform policy? They are definitely impacted. How about a new school-wide program for teaching mathematics? Yep, since parents and families will be trying to help their kids with their homework. What about funding amounts for different school programs? Probably not, since parents and families don't know all of the information about the budgeting context.

Would school leaders have to use all of the suggestions parents and families make on an issue? No. This is a collaboration. Leaders would use those suggestions to make the best policies they could. However, school leaders would be wise to show how they hope to use parents' feedback, as well as how they've used community feedback previously. In this way, leaders would draw from parents' power to support the school and help their children.

Now, what about something like a diversity program or a contentious curriculum program? These often attract the most publicity and create the most problems. Problems arise when schools don't seek feedback and increase when schools don't follow the feedback when it's aired through social media, school board meetings, protests to the school, and so forth. Sometimes school leaders choose to follow one constituency instead of another. These situations get ugly fast, sometimes leading to those extreme cases. In those extreme cases, leaders must decide if the program or policy is worth the price of not maximizing learning for all students.

WHAT'S THE TAKEAWAY?

It seems like schools go out of their way to try to remove or reduce obstacles to students' learning. After all, school leaders certainly want to increase students' learning. Schools spend thousands of dollars each year on programs, training, and materials in the hopes of increasing students' learning. Schools pay consultants to train teachers in new teaching methods. They try new assessment programs to gauge and stimulate students' learning. They tinker to find the most useful professional development approach for their teachers. They buy new laptops, tablets, or other teaching and learning devices.

But closer analysis reveals that this isn't quite true. Even with all of the attention, time, and money given to the task of improving students' learning, schools still maintain obstacles that impede this goal. These obstacles, though, are created by the schools. Well, perhaps they are not created, but they are certainly made to appear inherent, as if they're not actually obstacles: that school leaders don't seek input from all parties on all problems, that they don't open themselves for public criticism, that they usually don't try to predict the future, that they too often do a bad job of helping teachers teach to their strengths, and that they too often do school *to* students and families.

These are all obstacles to students' learning. Yet you might not think it, because it might not seem like these issues could even be addressed; they look as if that's just the way that schools are. What's worse is that many school leaders also likely don't see these issues as obstacles. But they are, and they all result from incorrect thinking about power. If power flowed from the top down, then it would make sense for school leaders to regulate who could contribute to problem solving. If some people held power but others did not, then it would make sense for only people with power to tackle big problems. But power doesn't work like that, so it doesn't make sense.

Following this reasoning, schools across the country tend to be run in ways that don't make sense. Consider this claim for a moment. Why would schools run by thousands of different people, all who received training from hundreds of different universities, education service centers, and other training sites, largely run schools in similar ways in relation to power? Two answers make the most sense: most people get power wrong, and that's just the way that schools are run—even if it's not the way that works best for students' learning.

This is the challenge for school leaders: to think about power as potential and to really truly do whatever it takes to help improve students' learning—even if you have to abandon ego or subject yourself to public criticism or even if you have to invite teachers and parents to help solve not just classroom-level problems but also system-level problems. This applies even if you have to work hard to try to predict the future or to find new ways to do school with students and families instead of to them.

To be clear, some schools do some of these things—but not enough. Too many schools still see power as a thing, as something linear, as a quality some people possess more than others. How can you know this? Just look at the actions. School leaders who think correctly about power will run schools differently. It is kind of like the "force" in the *Star Wars* movies; power is always there. It always is already acting like a web. To ignore it is to ignore the reality of power. The wisest school leaders will recognize this and strive to work with power to maximize students' learning.

NOTES

1. Elliot W. Eisner, *The educational imagination: On the design and evaluation of school programs*, 3rd ed. (Upper Saddle River, NJ: Prentice Hall, 2002).
2. Mary M. Kennedy, "Against boldness," *Journal of Teacher Education* 61, no. 1–2 (January 2010): 19.
3. Annette B. Weinshank, Emily S. Trumbull, and Patrick L. Daly, "The role of the teacher in school change," in *Handbook of teaching and policy*, ed. Lee S. Shulman and Gary Sykes (New York: Longman, 1983), 307.
4. Brad Olsen and Dena Sexton, "Threat rigidity, school reform, and how teachers view their work inside current education policy contexts," *American Educational Research Journal* 46, no. 1 (2008): 9.
5. Nelson Mandela, *Long walk to freedom: The autobiography of Nelson Mandela* (Boston: Back Bay Books, 1994).
6. Lee Ross, "The intuitive psychologist and his shortcomings: Distortions in the attribution process," in *Advances in experimental social psychology*, vol. 10, ed. Leonard Berkowitz (New York: Academic, 1977), 173–220.
7. Kennedy, "Against boldness," 20.
8. Jacob W. Neumann, "Examining mandated testing, teachers' milieu, and teachers' knowledge and beliefs: Gaining a fuller understanding of the web of influence on teachers' classroom practices," *Teachers College Record* 118, no. 2 (February 2016): 2.
9. Richard M. Ingersoll, *Who controls teachers' work? Power and accountability in America's schools* (Cambridge, MA: Harvard University Press, 2003).
10. Ray Dalio, *Principles* (New York: Simon & Schuster, 2017).
11. Dalio, *Principles*, 320.
12. Dalio, *Principles*, 303.
13. Dalio, *Principles*, 183.
14. Dalio, *Principles*, 371.
15. Clandinin and Connelly, "Teachers' professional knowledge landscapes: Teacher stories," 25.
16. Ludwig von Bertalanffy, *General systems theory: A new approach to unity of science* (Baltimore, MD: Johns Hopkins Press, 1951).
17. Frank Betts, "How systems thinking applies to education," *Educational Leadership* 50, no. 3 (1992): 38.
18. Betts, "Systems thinking," 38.
19. Marjolein Cox, Jan Elen, and An Steegen, "The use of causal diagrams to foster systems thinking in geography education: Results of an intervention study," *Journal of Geography* 118, no. 6 (April 2019): 238; Seamus Delaney, Joseph Paul Ferguson, and Madeleine Schultz, "Exploring opportunities to incorporate systems thinking into secondary and tertiary chemistry education through practitioner practices," *International Journal of Science Education* 43, no. 16 (September 2021): 2618; Catherine E. Sanders et al., "Teaching systems thinking with hypothetical case scenarios: An exploration in agricultural education," *Journal of Agricultural Education* 63, no. 4 (December 2022): 135; and Ann M. Stalter and Amy Jauch, "Systems

thinking education in RN-BSN programs: A regional study," *Nurse Educator* 44, no. 2 (2019): 112.

20. John A. Cassell and Thomas Nelson, "Visions lost and dreams forgotten: Environmental education, systems thinking, and possible futures in American public schools," *Teacher Education Quarterly* 34, no. 4 (Fall 2010): 191.

21. Agnieszka Bates, "Transcending systems thinking in education reform: Implications for policy-makers and school leaders," *Journal of Education Policy* 28, no. 1 (2013): 38.

22. Jacob W. Neumann and Bryan Meadows, "Problematizing notions of decontextualized 'best practice,'" *Curriculum and Teaching Dialogue* 13, no. 1/2 (2011): 93.

23. Dan C. Lortie, *Schoolteacher: A sociological study* (Chicago: The University of Chicago Press, 1975).

24. Mary H. Metz, "Real school," 75–91.

25. Donald A. Schön, *The reflective practitioner: How professionals think in action* (New York: Basic Books, 1983).

26. Nicquel T. Ellis and Boris Sanchez, "Turmoil erupts in school district after claims that critical race theory and transgender policy are being pushed," *CNN*, June 24, 2021, https://www.cnn.com/2021/06/24/us/loudoun-county-school-board-meeting/index.html; and Christopher F. Rufo, "Twisted measure to silence voices of dissent at school board meetings—arrest them," *New York Post*, November 17, 2021, https://nypost.com/2021/11/17/twisted-measure-to-silence-voices-at-school-board-meetings-arrest-them/.

Bibliography

Abel, Millicent H., and Joanne Sewell. "Stress and burnout in rural and urban secondary school teachers." *The Journal of Educational Research* 92, no. 5 (1999): 287–93.
Adams, Gabrielle S., Benjamin A. Converse, Andrew H. Hales, and Leidy E. Klotz. "People systematically overlook subtractive changes." *Nature* 592 (April 2021): 258–61.
Adnot, Melissa, Thomas Dee, Veronica Katz, and James Wyckoff. "Teacher turnover, teacher quality, and student achievement in DCPS." National Bureau of Economic Research, Working Paper 21922, January 2016. http://www.nber.org/papers/w21922.
Agar, Michael H. *The professional stranger: An informal introduction to ethnography*. 2nd ed. Bingley, UK: Emerald Group Publishing, 2008.
Apple, Michael W. *Teachers and texts: A political economy of class and gender relations in education*. London: Routledge, 1986.
Apple, Michael W., and Susan Jungck. "You don't have to be a teacher to teach this unit: Teaching, technology, and control in the classroom." In *Understanding teacher development*, edited by Andy Hargreaves and Michael G. Fullan, 20–44. London: Cassell, 1996.
Aoki, Ted. "Beyond the half-life of curriculum and pedagogy." *One World* 27, no. 2 (1990): 3–10.
Arendt, Hannah. *On violence*. New York: Harcourt, Brace & World, 1970.
Ashton, Patricia T., and Rodman B. Webb. *Making a difference: Teachers' sense of efficacy and student achievement*. New York: Longman, 1986.
Au, Wayne. "High-stakes testing and curricular control: A qualitative metasynthesis." *Educational Researcher* 36, no. 5 (2007): 258–67.
Au, Wayne. "Teaching under the new Taylorism: High-stakes testing and the standardization of the 21st century curriculum." *Journal of Curriculum Studies* 43, no. 1 (2011): 25–45.
Ballet, Katrijn, and Geert Kelchtermans. "Struggling with workload: Primary teachers' experience of intensification." *Teaching and Teacher Education* 25, no. 8 (November 2009): 1150–57.

Ballet, Katrijn, Geert Kelchtermans, and John Loughran. "Beyond intensification towards a scholarship of practice: Analysing changes in teachers' work lives." *Teachers and Teaching: Theory and Practice* 12, no. 2 (2006): 209–29.

Bar, Moshe, ed. *Predictions in the brain: Using our past to generate a future.* New York: Oxford University Press, 2011.

Barksdale, Mary A, and Karen F. Thomas. "What's at stake in high-stakes testing? Teachers and parents speak out." *Journal of Teacher Education* 51, no. 5 (2000): 384–97.

Bates, Agnieszka. "Transcending systems thinking in education reform: Implications for policy-makers and school leaders." *Journal of Education Policy* 28, no. 1 (2013): 38–54.

Battilana, Julie, and Tiziana Casciaro. *Power for all: How it really works and why it's everyone's business.* New York: Simon & Schuster, 2021.

Beaton, Caroline. "Humans are bad at predicting futures that don't benefit them." *The Atlantic*, November, 2, 2017. https://www.theatlantic.com/science/archive/2017/11/humans-are-bad-at-predicting-futures-that-dont-benefit-them/544709/.

Bergson, Henri. *Creative evolution.* New York: Philosophical Library, 1946.

Berliner, David C. "The near impossibility of testing for teacher quality." *Journal of Teacher Education* 56, no. 3 (2005): 205–13.

Betoret, Fernando D. "Stressors, self-efficacy, coping resources, and burnout among secondary school teachers in Spain." *Educational Psychology* 26 (2006): 519–39.

Betts, Frank. "How systems thinking applies to education." *Educational Leadership* 50, no. 3 (1992): 38–41.

Bierce, Ambrose. *The devil's dictionary.* New York: World Publishing Company, 1911.

Boskamp, Elsie. "25+ crucial average costs per hire facts [2023]: All cost of hiring Statistics." *Zippia* (blog), February 16, 2023. https://www.zippia.com/advice/cost-of-hiring-statistics-average-cost-per-hire/.

Britzman, Deborah P. "Cultural myths in the making of a teacher: Biography and social structure in teacher education." *Harvard Educational Review* 56, no. 4 (December 1986): 442–56.

Buescher, Thomas M. "A framework for understanding the social and emotional development of gifted and talented adolescents." *Roeper Review* 8, no. 1 (1985): 10–15.

Bui, Quoctrung, and Conor Dougherty. "Good schools, affordable homes: Finding the suburban sweet spots." *New York Times*, March 30, 2017. https://www.nytimes.com/interactive/2017/03/30/upshot/good-schools-affordable-homes-suburban-sweet-spots.html.

Campbell, R. J., and S. R. Neill. *Primary teachers at work.* London: Routledge, 1994.

Carman, Carol. "Comparing apples and oranges: Fifteen years of definitions of giftedness in research." *Journal of Advanced Academics* 24, no. 1 (February 2013): 52–70.

Cassell, John A., and Thomas Nelson. "Visions lost and dreams forgotten: Environmental education, systems thinking, and possible futures in American public schools." *Teacher Education Quarterly* 34, no. 4 (Fall 2010): 179–97.

Chappell, Bill. "A Texas lawmaker is targeting 850 books that he says could make students feel uneasy." NPR, Published October 28, 2021. https://www.npr.org/2021/10/28/1050013664/texas-lawmaker-matt-krause-launches-inquiry-into-850-books.

Cimbricz, Sandra. "State-mandated testing and teachers' beliefs and practices." *Education Policy Analysis Archives* 10, no. 2 (2002). http://epaa.asu.edu/epaa.v10n2.html.

Clandinin, D. Jean. *Classroom practice: Teacher images in action*. Philadelphia: Falmer Press, 1986.

Clandinin, D. Jean. "Narrative and story in teacher education." In *Teachers and teaching: From class to reflection*, edited by Tom Russell and Hugh Munby, 124–37. Philadelphia: Falmer Press, 1992.

Clandinin, D. Jean, and F. Michael Connelly. *Teachers' professional knowledge landscapes*. New York: Teachers College Press, 1995.

Clandinin, D. Jean, and F. Michael Connelly. "Teachers' professional knowledge landscapes: Teacher stories. Stories of teachers. School stories. Stories of school." *Educational Researcher* 25, no. 3 (1996): 24–30.

Coleman, Laurence J., and Michael D. Sanders. "Understanding the needs of gifted students: Social needs, social choices and masking one's giftedness." *Journal of Secondary Gifted Education* 5, no. 1 (January 1993): 22–25.

Coleman, Laurence J., and Tracey L. Cross. "Is being gifted a social handicap?" *Journal for the Education of the Gifted* 11, no. 4 (July 1988): 41–56.

Connelly, F. Michael, and D. Jean Clandinin. "Narrative understandings of teacher knowledge." *Journal of Curriculum and Supervision* 15, no. 4 (Summer 2000): 315–31.

Connelly, F. Michael, and D. Jean Clandinin. "Stories of experience and narrative inquiry." *Educational Researcher* 19, no. 5 (1990): 2–14.

Corbin, Juliet, and Anselm Strauss. *Basics of qualitative research*. 3rd ed. Los Angeles: Sage, 2008.

Counts, George S. *Dare the school build a new social order?* Carbondale, IL: Southern Illinois University Press, 1978.

Cox, Marjolein, Jan Elen, and An Steegen. "The use of causal diagrams to foster systems thinking in geography education: Results of an intervention study." *Journal of Geography* 118, no. 6 (April 2019): 238–51.

Craig, Cheryl J. "'Butterfly under a pin': An emergent teacher image amid mandated curriculum reform." *The Journal of Educational Research* 105, no. 2 (February 2012): 90–101.

Craig, Cheryl J. "Coming to know in the 'eye of the storm': A beginning teacher's introduction to different versions of teacher community." *Teaching and Teacher Education* 29 (January 2013): 25–38.

Craig, Cheryl J. "The contested classroom space: A decade of lived educational policy in Texas schools." *American Educational Research Journal* 46, no. 4 (December 2009): 1034–59.

Craig, Cheryl J. "The dragon in school backyards: The influence of mandated testing on school contexts and educators' narrative knowing." *Teachers College Record* 106, no. 6 (June 2004): 1229–57.

Craig, Cheryl J. "The influence of context on one teacher's interpretive knowledge of team teaching." *Teaching and Teacher Education* 14, no. 4 (1998): 371–83.

Craig, Cheryl J. "The relationship between and among teachers' narrative knowledge, communities of knowing, and school reform: A case of 'The Monkey's Paw.'" *Curriculum Inquiry* 31, no. 3 (2001): 303–31.

Craig, Cheryl J. "Stories of schools/teacher stories: A two-part invention on the walls theme."

Curriculum Inquiry 30, no. 1 (2000): 11–41.Crocco, Margaret S., and Arthur T. Costigan. "High-stakes teaching: What's at stake for teachers (and students) in the age of accountability?" *The New Educator* 2, no. 1 (January 2006): 1–13.

Cross, Tracey L., Laurence J. Coleman, and Marge Terhaar-Yonkers. "The social cognition of gifted adolescents in schools: Managing the stigma of giftedness." *Journal for the Education of the Gifted* 15, no. 1 (October 1991): 44–55.

Cross, Tracey L., Laurence J. Coleman, and Roger A. Stewart. "The social cognition of gifted adolescents: An exploration of the stigma of giftedness paradigm." *Roeper Review* 16, no. 1 (1993): 37–40.Csikszentmihaly, Mihaly. *The evolving self: A psychology for the third millennium.* New York: Harper Perennial, 1993.

Cuban, Larry. "Constancy and change in schools (1880s to the present)." In *Contributing to educational change: Perspectives on research and practice,* edited by Philip W. Jackson, 85–105. Berkeley, CA: McCutchan Publishing Company, 1988.

Cuban, Larry. "Hugging the middle: Teaching in an era of testing and accountability, 1980–2005." *Education Policy Analysis Archives* 15, no. 1 (January 2007): 1–27.

Cuban, Larry. "The lure of curricular reform and its pitiful history." *Phi Delta Kappan* 75, no. 2 (October 1993): 182–85.

Cuban, Larry. "Persistent instruction: Another look at constancy in the classroom." *Phi Delta Kappan* 68, no. 1 (September 1986): 7–11.

Cuban, Larry. "Persistent instruction: The high school classroom." *Phi Delta Kappan* 64, no. 2 (October 1982): 113–18. Dai, David Y. "Essential tensions surrounding the concept of giftedness." In *International handbook of giftedness*, edited by Larissa Shavinina, 39–80. Houten, The Netherlands: Springer, 2009.

Dai, David Y. *The nature and nurture of giftedness: A new framework for understanding gifted education.* New York: Teachers College Press, 2010.

Dalio, Ray. *Principles.* New York: Simon & Schuster, 2017.

Davis, Gary A., and Sylvia B. Rimm. *Education of the gifted and talented.* 5th ed. Boston: Allyn & Bacon, 2004.

Delaney, Seamus, Joseph Paul Ferguson, and Madeleine Schultz. "Exploring opportunities to incorporate systems thinking into secondary and tertiary chemistry education through practitioner practices." *International Journal of Science Education* 43, no. 16 (September 2021): 2618–39.

Densmore, Kathleen. "Professionalism, proletarianization, and teachers' work." In *Critical studies in teacher education,* edited by Thomas Popkewitz, 130–60. London: Falmer Press, 1987.

Dweck, Carol S. "Mindsets and human nature: Promoting change in the Middle East, the schoolyard, the racial divide, and willpower." *American Psychologist* 67, no. 8 (November 2012): 614–22.

Dweck, Carol S. *Mindset: The new psychology for success*. New York: Ballantine Books, 2006.

Easthope, Chris, and Gary Easthope. "Intensification, extension, and complexity of teachers' workload." *British Journal of Sociology of Education* 21, no. 1 (March 2000): 43–58.

Eiser, J. Richard, and Christine Eiser. "Prediction of environmental change: Wish-fulfillment revisited." *European Journal of Social Psychology* 5, no. 3 (1975): 315–22.

Eisner, Elliot W. *The educational imagination: On the design and evaluation of school programs*. 3rd ed. Upper Saddle River, NJ: Prentice Hall, 2002.

Ellis, Nicquel T., and Boris Sanchez. "Turmoil erupts in school district after claims that critical race theory and transgender policy are being pushed." *CNN*, June 24, 2021. https://www.cnn.com/2021/06/24/us/loudoun-county-school-board-meeting/index.html.

Faulkner, Shawn A., and Christopher M. Cook. "Testing vs. teaching: The perceived impact of assessment demands on middle grades instructional practices." *Research in Middle Level Education Online* 29, no. 7 (January 2006): 1–13.

Feiker Hollenbeck, Amy R. "Beyond talking about books: Implications of the reading comprehension instruction and pedagogical beliefs of a special educator perceived as effective." *Learning Disability Quarterly* 36, no. 2 (April 2013): 112–25.

Feldhusen, John F., and David Y. Dai. "Gifted students' attitudes and perceptions of the gifted label, special programs, and peer relations." *Journal of Secondary Gifted Education* 9, no. 1 (August 1997): 15–20.

Firestone, William A., Lora Monfils, Gregory Camilli, Roberta Schorr, Jennifer Hicks, and David Mayrowetz. "The ambiguity of test preparation: A multimethod analysis in one state." *Teachers College Record* 104, no. 7 (October 2002): 1485–523.

Fischler, Jacob. "What parents need to know about school vouchers." *U.S. News & World Report*, October 22, 2021. https://www.usnews.com/education/k12/articles/what-parents-need-to-know-about-school-vouchers.

Folger, Robert, and Mary A. Konovsky. "Effects of procedural and distributive justice on reactions to pay raise decisions." *Academy of Management Journal* 32, no. 1 (March 1989): 115–30.

Foucault, Michel. *The history of sexuality: An introduction*. Vol. 1. Translated by Robert Hurley. New York: Vintage Books, 1990.

Foucault, Michel. *Power*. Edited by James D. Faubion. New York: The New Press, 2000.

Garcia, Emma, and Elaine Weiss. *Examining the factors that play a role in the teacher shortage crisis: Key findings from EPI's 'Perfect Storm in the Teacher Labor Market' series*. Washington, DC: Economic Policy Institute, 2020. https://files.eric.ed.gov/fulltext/ED611183.pdf.

Gaylor, K. *How have high school exit exams changed our schools? Some perspectives from Virginia and Maryland*. Washington, DC: Center on Educational Policy, 2005.

Gibson, Sherri, and Myron H. Dembo. "Teacher efficacy: A construct validation." *Journal of Educational Psychology* 76 (August 1984): 569–82.

Gitlin, Andrew. "Bounding teacher decision making: The threat of intensification." *Educational Policy* 15, no. 2 (May 2001): 227–57.

Glassdoor Team. "How to calculate cost-per-hire." *Glassdoor for Employers* (blog), July 5, 2019. https://www.glassdoor.com/employers/blog/calculate-cost-per-hire/.

Graham, Suzanne, Tony MacFadyen, and Brian Richards. "Learners' perceptions of being identified as very able: Insights from modern foreign languages and physical education." *Journal of Curriculum Studies* 44, no. 3 (May 2012): 323–48.

Grant, S. G. "An uncertain lever: Exploring the influence of state-level testing in New York State on teaching social studies." *Teachers College Record* 103, no. 3 (April 2001): 398–426.

Grant, S. G. *History lessons: Teaching, learning, and testing in United States high school classrooms.* Mahwah, NJ: Lawrence Erlbaum Associates, 2003.

Grant, S. G. *Measuring history: Cases of state-level testing across the United States.* Greenwich, CT: Information Age Publishing, 2006.

Grossman, Pam L., Suzanne M. Wilson, and Lee S. Shulman. "Teachers of substance: Subject matter knowledge for teaching." In *Knowledge base for the beginning teacher*, edited by Maynard C. Reynolds, 23–36. New York: Pergamon, 1989.

Guskin, Samuel L., Cynthia Okolo, Enid Zimmerman, and Chao-Ying J. Peng. "Being labeled gifted or talented: Meanings and effects perceived by students in special programs." *Gifted Child Quarterly* 3, no. 2 (Spring 1986): 61–65.

Habermas, Jurgen, and Thomas McCarthy. "Hannah Arendt's communications concept of power." *Social Research* 44, no. 1 (Spring 1977): 3–24.

Hansen, David T. "A poetics of teaching." *Educational Theory* 54, no. 2 (April 2004): 119–42.

Hanushek, Eric A., Steven G. Rivkin, and Jeffrey C. Schiman. "Dynamic effects of teacher turnover on the quality of instruction." *Economics of Education Review* 55 (2016): 132–48.

Hargreaves, Andy. *Changing teachers, changing times: Teachers' work and culture in the postmodern age.* New York: Teachers College Press, 1994.

Hargreaves, Andy. "Time and teachers' work: An analysis of the intensification thesis." *Teachers College Record* 94, no. 1 (1992): 87–108.

Hayes, Samuel P. "The predictive ability of voters." *Journal of Social Psychology* 7 (1936): 183–90.

Henry, Gary T., and Christopher Redding. "The consequences of leaving school early: The effects of within-year and end-of-year teacher turnover." *Education Finance & Policy* 15, no. 2 (2018): 332–56.

Hoge, Robert D., and Joseph S. Renzulli. "Exploring the link between giftedness and self-concept." *Review of Educational Research* 63, no. 4 (Winter 1993): 449–65.

Impelli, Matthew, "McAuliffe saying parents shouldn't tell schools what to teach big factor in election: Poll." *Newsweek*, November 5, 2021. https://www.newsweek.com/mcauliffe-saying-parents-shouldnt-tell-schools-what-teach-big-factor-election-poll-1649488.

Ingersoll, Richard M. *Who controls teachers' work? Power and accountability in America's schools.* Cambridge, MA: Harvard University Press, 2003.

Ittelson, William H., and Hadley Cantril. *Perception: A transactional approach.* New York: Doubleday & Co., 1954.

Jones, M. Gail, Brett D. Jones, Belinda Hardin, Lisa Chapman, Tracie Yarbrough, and Marcia Davis. "The impact of high-stakes testing on teachers and students in North Carolina." *Phi Delta Kappan* 8, no. 3 (November 1999): 199–203.

Jones, M. Gail, Brett. D. Jones, and Tracy Y. Hargrove. *The unintended consequences of high-stakes testing.* Lanham, MD: Rowman & Littlefield, 2003.

Kagan, Dona M. "Implications of research on teacher belief." *Educational Psychologist* 27, no. 1 (1992): 65–90.

Kagan, Dona M., and Kenneth E. Smith. "Beliefs and behaviors of kindergarten teachers." *Educational Researcher* 30, no. 1 (1988): 26–35.

Kennedy, Mary M. "Against boldness." *Journal of Teacher Education* 61, no. 1–2 (January 2010): 16–20.

Kennedy, Mary M. *Inside teaching: How classroom life undermines reform.* Cambridge, MA: Harvard University Press, 2005.

Kennedy, Mary M. "Knowledge and vision in teaching." *Journal of Teacher Education* 57, no. 3 (May 2006): 205–11.

Kerr, Barbara, Nicholas Colangelo, and Julie Gaeth. "Gifted adolescents' attitudes toward their giftedness." *Gifted Child Quarterly* 3, no. 2 (April 1988): 245–47.

Klotz, Leidy. *Subtract: The untapped science of less.* New York: Flatiron Books, 2021.

Kunkel, Mark A., Beatrice M. Chapa, Greg Patterson, and Derald Walling. "The experience of giftedness: A concept map." *Gifted Child Quarterly* 39, no. 3 (July 1995): 126–34.

Larson, Sarfatti. "Proletarianization and educated labor." *Theory and Society* 9, no. 1 (January 1980): 131–75.

Litt, Mark D., and Dennis C. Turk. "Sources of stress and dissatisfaction in experienced high school teachers." *Journal of Educational Research* 78, no. 3 (1985): 178–85.

Lopez, Brian. "It's not just Covid-19: Why Texas faces a teacher shortage." *The Texas Tribune*, July 25, 2022. https://www.texastribune.org/2022/07/25/texas-teacher-shortage/.

Lortie, Dan C. *Schoolteacher: A sociological study.* Chicago: The University of Chicago Press, 1975.

Lund, Frederick H. "The psychology of belief." *Journal of Abnormal and Social Psychology* 20 (1925): 23–81.

Machiavelli, Niccolo. *The prince.* Translated by George Bull. London: Penguin Classics, 2003.

Makel, Matthew C., Kate E. Snyder, Chandler Thomas, Patrick S. Malone, and Martha Putallaz. "Gifted students' implicit beliefs about intelligence and giftedness." *Gifted Child Quarterly* 59, no. 4 (August 2015): 202–13.

Mandela, Nelson. *Long walk to freedom: The autobiography of Nelson Mandela.* Boston: Back Bay Books, 1994.

Manor-Bullock, Rochelle, Christine Look, and David N. Dixon. "Is giftedness socially stigmatizing? The impact of high achievement on social interactions." *Journal for the Education of the Gifted* 18, no. 3 (July 1995): 319–38.

Marsh, Herbert W., Danuta Chessor, Rhonda Craven, and Lawrence Roche. "The effects of gifted and talented programs on academic self-concept: The big fish strikes again." *American Educational Research Journal* 32, no. 2 (Summer 1995): 285–319.

McNeil, Linda. *Contradictions of school reform: Educational costs of standardized testing*. New York: Routledge, 2000.

Meadows, Bryan, and Jacob W. Neumann. "What does it mean to assess gifted students' perceptions of giftedness labels?" *Interchange* 48, no. 2 (May 2017): 145–65.

Mehan, Hugh. "The construction of an LD student: A case study in the politics of representation." In *Discourse theory and practice: A reader*, edited by Margaret Wetherell, Stephanie Taylor, and Simeon Yates, 345–63. London: Sage, 2001.

Metz, Mary H. "Real school: A universal drama amid disparate experience." In *Education politics for a new century*, edited by Douglas E. Mitchell and Margaret E. Goertz, 75–91. Bristol, PA: The Falmer Press, 1989.

Mudrak, Jiri, and Katerina Zabrodska. "Childhood giftedness, adolescent agency: A systemic multiple-case study." *Gifted Child Quarterly* 59, no. 1 (November 2014): 55–70.

Neumann, Jacob W. "Examining mandated testing, teachers' milieu, *and* teachers' knowledge and beliefs: Gaining a fuller understanding of the web of influence on teachers' classroom practices." *Teachers College Record* 118, no. 2 (February 2016): 1–50.

Neumann, Jacob W. "Teaching to and beyond the test: The influence of mandated accountability testing on one social studies teacher's classroom." *Teachers College Record* 115, no. 6 (2013): 1–32.

Neumann, Jacob W., and Bryan Meadows. "Problematizing notions of decontextualized 'best practice.'" *Curriculum and Teaching Dialogue* 13, no. 1/2 (2011): 93–107.

Newmann, Fred M. "Can depth replace coverage in the high school curriculum?" *Phi Delta Kappan* 69, no. 5 (January 1988): 345–48.

Newmann, Fred M. "Higher order thinking in teaching social studies: A rationale for the assessment of classroom thoughtfulness." *Journal of Curriculum Studies* 22, no. 1 (1990): 41–56.

Nickerson, Raymond S. "Confirmation bias: A ubiquitous phenomenon in many guises." *Review of General Psychology* 2, no. 2 (June 1998): 175–220.

Nietzsche, Friedrich. *The will to power*. Translated by Walter Kaufmann and R. J. Hollingdale. Edited by Walter Kaufmann. New York: Vintage Books, 1967.

Olsen, Brad, and Dena Sexton. "Threat rigidity, school reform, and how teachers view their work inside current education policy contexts." *American Educational Research Journal* 46, no. 1 (2008): 9–44.

Papay, John J., and Matthew A. Kraft. "The productivity costs of inefficient hiring practices: Evidence from late teacher hiring." *Journal of Policy Analysis and Management* 35, no. 4 (June 2016): 791–817.

Parsons, Talcott. "On the concept of political power." In *Politics and social structure*, edited by Talcott Parsons, 352–404. New York: Free Press, 1969.
Parsons, Talcott. *Structure and process in modern societies*. Glencoe, IL: Free Press, 1960. Pearson, Donna. "CTE and the Common Core can address the problem of silos." *Phi Delta Kappan* 96, no. 6 (February 2015): 12–16.
Penta, Leo J. "Hannah Arendt: On power." *The Journal of Speculative Philosophy* 10, no. 3 (1996): 210–29.
Reid, William A. "Curriculum as institutionalized learning: Implications for theory and research." *Journal of Curriculum and Supervision* 19, no. 1 (Fall 2003): 29–43.
Richardson, Virginia, Patricia Anders, Deborah Tidwell, and Carol Loyd. "The relationship between teachers' beliefs and practices in reading comprehension instruction." *American Educational Research Journal* 28, no. 3 (1991): 559–86.
Robinson, Amy. "Does that describe me? Adolescents' acceptance of the gifted label." *Journal for the Education of the Gifted* 13 (1990): 245–55.
Rockoff, Jonah E., and Cecilia Speroni. "Subjective and objective evaluations of teacher effectiveness." *The American Economic Review* 100, no. 2 (May 2010): 261–66.
Ronfeldt, Matthew, Hamilton Lankford, Susanna Loeb, and James Wyckoff. "How teacher turnover harms student achievement." National Bureau of Economic Research, Working Paper 17176, June 2011. http://www.nber.org/papers/w17176.
Ross, Lee. "The intuitive psychologist and his shortcomings: Distortions in the attribution process." In *Advances in experimental social psychology*, vol. 10, edited by Leonard Berkowitz, 173–220. New York: Academic, 1977.
Rothwell, Jonathan. "Housing costs, zoning, and access to high-scoring schools." Brookings Institution. Published April 19, 2012. https://www.brookings.edu/research/housing-costs-zoning-and-access-to-high-scoring-schools/.
Rufo, Christopher F. "Twisted measure to silence voices of dissent at school board meetings—arrest them." *New York Post*, November 17, 2021. https://nypost.com/2021/11/17/twisted-measure-to-silence-voices-at-school-board-meetings-arrest-them/.
Russell, Bertrand. *Power*. London: Routledge Classics, 2004.
Salinas, Cynthia. "Teaching in a high-stakes testing setting." In *Measuring history: Cases of state-level testing across the United States*, edited by S. G. Grant, 177–93. Charlotte, NC: Information Age Publishing, 2006.
Sanders, Catherine E., Allison R. Fortner, Kristin E. Gibson, Kevan W. Lamm, and Alexa J. Lamm. "Teaching systems thinking with hypothetical case scenarios: An exploration in agricultural education." *Journal of Agricultural Education* 63, no. 4 (December 2022): 135–50.
Scharlach, Tabatha D. "These kids just aren't motivated to read: The influence of preservice teachers' beliefs on their expectations, instruction, and evaluation of struggling readers." *Literacy research and instruction* 47, no. 1 (2008): 58–173.
Schön, Donald A. *The reflective practitioner: How professionals think in action*. New York: Basic Books, 1983.
Schwab, Joseph J. "The practical 4: Something for curriculum professors to do." *Curriculum Inquiry* 13, no. 3 (1983): 239–65.

Silin, Jonathan G., and Fran Schwartz. "Staying close to the teacher." *Teachers College Record* 105, no. 8 (October 2003): 1586–605.

Smith, Mary L. "Put to the test: The effects of external testing on teachers." *Educational Researcher* 20, no. 5 (June 1991): 8–11.

Soll, Ivan. "Nietzsche's will to power as a psychological thesis." *Journal of Nietzsche Studies* 43, no. 1 (Spring 2012): 118–29.

Soll, Ivan. "Nietzsche disempowered: Reading the will to power out of Nietzsche's philosophy." *Journal of Nietzsche Studies* 46, no. 3 (Autumn 2015): 425–50.

Soodak, Leslie C., and David M. Podell. "Teachers' thinking about difficult-to-teach students." *Journal of Educational Research* 88, no. 1 (September–October 1994): 44–51.

Stalter, Ann M., and Amy Jauch. "Systems thinking education in RN-BSN programs: A regional study." *Nurse Educator* 44, no. 2 (2019): 112–15.

Staubmann, Helmut. "C. Wright Mills' The sociological imagination and the construction of Talcott Parsons as a conservative grand theorist." *The American Sociologist* 52 (March 2021): 178–93.

Sutton, Robert I. "Why bosses should ask employers to do less—not more." *Wall Street Journal*, September, 25, 2022. https://www.wsj.com/articles/bosses-staff-employees-less-work-11663790432?mod=Searchresults_pos1&page=1.

Terman, Lewis M. *Genetic studies of genius: Mental and physical traits of a thousand gifted children*. Stanford, CA: Stanford University Press, 1926.

Texas Education Agency. "Career and Technology Funding Allotment." N.d. https://tea.texas.gov/finance-and-grants/state-funding/additional-finance-resources/career-and-technology-education-allotment.

Texas Education Agency. "Employed teacher attrition and new hires 2011–12 through 2022–23." Published March 2023. https://tea.texas.gov/sites/default/files/employed-teacher-attrition-and-new-hires.pdf.

Texas Education Agency. "Funding for CTE." Accessed on April 5, 2023. https://texasgateway.org/resource/lesson-4-cte-funding-and-attendance-accounting?binder_id=124791.

Texas Education Agency. "STAAR Executive Summary." Published 2010. www.tea.state.tx.us/student.assessment/hb3/HB3-ExecutiveSummary.pdf.

Texas Education Agency. "STAAR to replace TAKS." Published 2010. http://www.tea.state.tx.us/index4.aspx?id=7874.

Texas Education Agency. "Teacher retention by preparation route 2011–12 through 2021–22." Published March 2023. https://tea.texas.gov/sites/default/files/teacher-retention-by-preparation-route.pdf.Tyack, David, and Larry Cuban. *Tinkering toward utopia: A century of public school reform*. Cambridge, MA: Harvard University Press, 1995.

Tyack, David, and William Tobin. "The 'grammar' of schooling: Why has it been so hard to change?" *American Education Research Journal* 31, no. 3 (1994): 453–79.

Valli, Linda, and Daria Buese. "The changing roles of teachers in an era of high-stakes accountability." *American Educational Research Journal* 44, no. 3 (2007): 519–58.

van Manen, Max. "Phenomenological pedagogy." *Curriculum Inquiry* 12, no. 3 (Autumn 1982): 283–99.

Vansledright, Bruce A., and S. G. Grant. "Citizenship education and the persistent nature of classroom teaching dilemmas." *Theory and Research in Social Education* 22, no. 3 (Summer 1994): 305–39.

Vogler, Kenneth. E. "Comparing the impact of accountability examinations on Mississippi and Tennessee social studies teachers' instructional practices." *Educational Assessment* 13, no. 1 (April 2008): 1–32.

Vogler, Kenneth. E. "Impact of a high school graduation examination on social studies teachers' instructional practices." *Journal of Social Studies Research* 29, no. 2 (2005): 19–33.

Vogler, Kenneth E. "The impact of high-stakes, state-mandated student performance assessment on teachers' instructional practices." *Education* 123, no. 1 (September 2002): 39–55.

Vogler, Kenneth E., and David Virtue. "'Just the facts, ma'am': Teaching social studies in the era of standards and high-stakes testing." *The Social Studies* 98, no. 2 (2007): 54–58.

von Bertalanffy, Ludwig. *General systems theory: A new approach to unity of science*. Baltimore, MD: Johns Hopkins Press, 1951.

Weber, Max. *Economy and society*. Translated by Guenther Roth and Claus Wittich. Berkeley, CA: University of California Press, 1978.

Weinshank, Annette B., Emily S. Trumbull, and Patrick L. Daly. "The role of the teacher in school change." In *Handbook of teaching and policy*, edited by Lee S. Shulman and Gary Sykes, 300–14. New York: Longman, 1983.

Weinstein, Neil D. "Unrealistic optimism about future life events." *Journal of Personality and Social Psychology* 39, no. 5 (November 1980): 806–20.

Williamson, Pamela, Elizabeth Bondy, Lisa Langley, and Dina Mayne. "Meeting the challenge of high-stakes testing while remaining child-centered: The representations of two urban teachers." *Childhood Education* 81, no. 4 (2005): 190–95.

Wills, John S. "Putting the squeeze on social studies: Managing teaching dilemmas in subject areas excluded from state testing." *Teachers College Record* 109, no. 8 (August 2007): 1980–2046.

Wills, John S., and Judith H. Sandholtz. "Constrained professionalism: Dilemmas of teaching in the face of test-based accountability." *Teachers College Record* 111, no. 4 (April 2009): 1065–1114.

Wilson, Suzanne M., and Samuel S. Wineburg. "Peering at history through different lenses: The role of disciplinary perspectives in teaching history." *Teachers College Record* 89, no. 4 (Summer 1988): 525–39.

About the Author

Jacob W. Neumann, EdD, is professor of curriculum and instruction at the University of Texas Rio Grande Valley. Dr. Neumann currently teaches in the doctoral program for curriculum and instruction, and he previously taught in the university's undergraduate teacher-preparation program. Dr. Neumann has taught at all levels of schooling: elementary, middle, and high school, as well as community college and university. His research has been published in journals such as *Teachers College Record*, *Educational Theory*, and *Phi Delta Kappan*.

www.ingramcontent.com/pod-product-compliance
Lightning Source LLC
Chambersburg PA
CBHW020124010526
44115CB00008B/956